TESTI

MOTHERI

AND ALL THA

This book is like having coffee with your best friend who added 'just a touch' of tequila, because it's the right thing for right now. Shared with empathy, understanding and downright realness, you're about to discover the recipe for successful momma entrepreneurs.

Mike Michalowicz

Author of *Profit First* (and a wannabe momma entrepreneur)

Cyndi's insights into our daily challenges as business owners and parents, left me feeling safe, comfortable and "normal". There were many days over the last 10 years that I felt very alone in my dual roles. I see now that I was never really alone. We are all navigating this adventure together, with its great days and its struggles. Thank you, Cyndi, for highlighting us and showing so many other parents that they also are not alone.

Wendy Barlin CPA

Author of *Never Budget Again, That's Deductible!*

Taking the leap from my stable, 9-5, corporate career to being a business owner (as a brand new mom) was terrifying! My financial stability, routine, and predictable life was all going to be out the window. Cyndi Thomason's book, *Motherhood, Apple Pie, and All That Happy Horseshit,* is not only a realistic look at how my new life could be, but also a guide to follow as I grow my business while raising my boys. It's a map and confidence builder that should motivate every mom with an idea to take the next step and turn her dream into a reality!

Beth Fynbo CEO

Inventor and Boss Mom at Busy Baby

I left my job and started my business to have the freedom to be there for my children as they grow up. I make intentional choices to design my business so that I have the opportunity to be there for my children in ways that matter most to them and me. It is possible to have a business that supports your life, not the other way around! In *Motherhood, Apple Pie, and All That Happy Horseshit,* Cyndi lays out the guiding principles and a clear path to doing so.

Sabrina Starling, PhD
Author of *The 4 Week Vacation®*

Being a mom-prenuer, should not be about having to choose between your career and your kids. It's about finding the balance to succeed in both. In this must-read book, Cyndi Thomason lays out a framework for designing a successful business that gives you the control and the focus to also design the life you (and your kids) deserve.

Sara Nay
COO at Duct Tape Marketing
and Founder of Spark Lab Consulting

The day we left the hospital after my son was born, I remember wishing the hospital staff had tucked an instructional guide in with the diapers. I understood the worlds of business and leadership and had no shortage of confidence in those arenas. But as a new mom, I could feel self-doubt creep up the back of my neck as we neared home. Did I have what it took to be an incredible mom to this beautiful child? And later, how could I balance the demands of entrepreneurship while caring exceptionally well for him?

How I wish I had had Cyndi Thomason's *Motherhood, Apple Pie, and All That Happy Horseshit* then!

In this must-read guide for mothers who are wanting to reclaim their lives without sacrificing quality time with their family or attention paid to their business, Cyndi Thomason shows women how to put their dreams first, get the help they need, and model desired values to their children—all while building the enterprise of their dreams.

Susie deVille

Author of *Buoyant: The Entrepreneur's Guide to Becoming Wildly Successful, Creative, and Free*

Being a mom entrepreneur is tough but Cyndi guides us to find a healthy balance so that we can actually enjoy it ALL! Cyndi is honest, practical, and loving but she won't let you off the hook for standing in your own way. This book will challenge you, heal you and move you forward. Saddle up, sisters. This is the REAL DEAL!

Kristin Ostrander

Founder of MommyIncome.com

Cyndi is a pioneer in the ecommerce industry with the ability to apply broader business concepts in a way that is actionable for new and seasoned entrepreneurs. Her new book explains in a super practical way, how moms can truly have it all, in business, family, and in their personal lives. A breath of fresh air, and a much-needed break for boss babes worldwide!

Amy Wees

Fellow Mom and Boss Babe

Founder of Amazing at Home E-Commerce Consulting

A very direct, honest and funny book that will give you lots to laugh about, but will also support and propel you to grow while your kids grow and feed your soul.

Tatiana Tsoir

Author of "Dream Bold, Start Smart: Be Your Own Boss and Make Money Doing What You Love"

If you are looking for a path to build a business that allows you to have a life that has both the success of owning your own business, but also the peace and freedom you want for your family, there is no one better to learn from than Cyndi Thomason. Cyndi is the living embodiment of everything in this book. She doesn't just give you theories, because she has done this for herself. She has created an amazingly successful business while still prioritizing time with her family. She has also let her business grow and change with the changing needs of her family.

You don't need something else to do. You are already busy enough. Cyndi is the person I would send someone to if they want to build something that supports and nurtures them and their family.

Robyn Johnson,

CEO and Founder, Marketplace Blueprint

This is a very down-to-fearth book, filled with love, support and real stories of moms who did it their way. These stories are inspiring and might give you some great practical tips along the way to do it your way too! I am proud some of my stories are in this book.

Femke Hogema

CEO Profit First Professionals BV (Netherlands)

Cyndi is a devoted mother, a masterful business woman, and a generous mentor. *Motherhood, Apple Pie, and All That Happy Horseshit* is the guidance I wish I had before I started it all.

Susanne Mariga, CPA

Author of *Profit First for Minority Business Enterprises*

FINALLY! A book to help our wonderful women be their best with ACTUAL strategies that are easy to implement, and without pulling punches about the complicated messiness of "real life" that women handle each day as part of their being real deal superheroes among us.

Steven Black

Founder of The Unstoppable Marketing Masterclass

As a mama building a business, you may feel like you've been flying high (but solo) for a little bit too long... and this book will be the warm blanket, comforting cup of tea, and profit-driven action plan you need to reconnect to the initial vision and drive that had you embark on the journey of entrepreneurship while raising tiny humans. Cyndi's wisdom and expertise will remind you: "Take the next step, and the next step, and the next step. The bridge will be there when you need it. Don't look back. Don't look down. Just take that step and fly." Just don't fly solo anymore. Take Cyndi along!

Kinia Romanowska

CEO, Pros&Babes: Where Careers and Families Grow Together

Motherhood, Apple Pie, and All That Happy Horseshit is a life-changing book that reads like a warm, honest conversation with your favorite friend, the one who never judges you and always has the best advice. This book helped me to make a critical decision that opened up my work schedule so I could do more of the work I love while I continue to grow my business and stay present for my family. A must-read for moms who want it all!

AJ Harper

Author of *Write a Must-Read*

MOTHERHOOD, APPLE PIE,

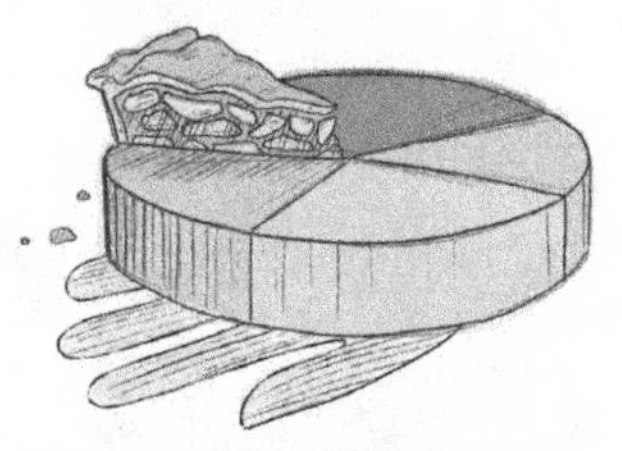

and all that HAPPY HORSESHIT

BUSINESS IS PERSONAL

CYNDI THOMASON

Motherhood, Apple Pie, and All That Happy Horseshit

bookskeep, 9004 Bear Creek Cv, Harrison, AR 72601
https://www.cyndithomason.com/

Printed in the United States of America

ISBN 13: 978-0-9600283-3-7 (trade paperback)
ISBN 13: 978-0-9600283-4-4 (audio file)
ISBN 13: 978-0-9600283-5-1 (ebook)

Cover and book design by CB Messer

10 9 8 7 6 5 4 3 2 1

I dedicate this book to my mom, Eleanor Potts, who taught me all the important lessons in making good choices as both a mom and an entrepreneur.

CONTENTS

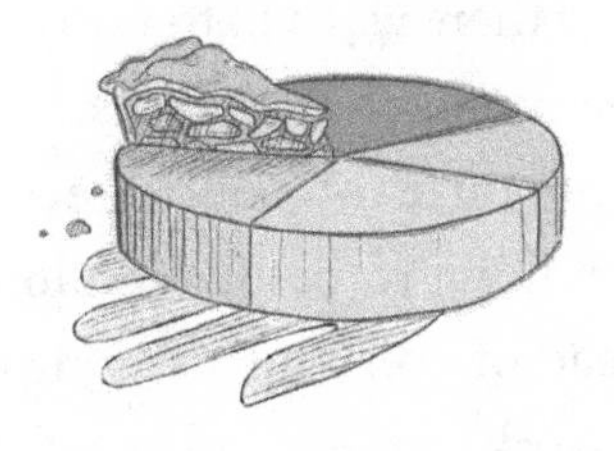

INTRODUCTION

My boss looked at me with eyes as big as saucers. He did not blink. From his reaction, I knew I was dancing at the edge of the cliff. Still, I went on with my passionate plea…

Less than an hour before, I had been sitting in my usual spot in the conference room, along the wall. Only my boss, the president of the company, sat at the table with the other board members.

Our small research firm met with our board every quarter. Most of the time, we were seeking approval for a technical research project and I wasn't too attached to the outcome. Today was different. I wanted the board's approval to move forward with restructuring the organization. I knew it was the right next step for the company *and* I knew it would be outside the board members' paradigms. Most of them were high-level executives in large electric utility companies, and their corporate world view of an organizational framework was limited to traditional hierarchies. Their experience had taught them that traditional organizational charts worked—for the company. I knew there was a better way: a way that would work for the company *and* its employees.

We wanted to organize into self-directed project teams and for decision-making to be pushed lower down in the organization. Instead of everyone working on solo projects, they would start to work together and benefit from the synergy of combining each other's experience and unique skills. The organization would become more collaborative; team members would work on multiple projects and be responsible for progress based on collective decisions. We were a team of professionals and wanted to set broad goals and manage the day-to-day without going through an approval process. The management team developed this new approach with lots of staff input. It gave them a lot of latitude, both in managing their professional networks and in setting up more flexible work schedules within their teams. Hoping for better work-life balance, the staff had been itching to move in this direction. I was invested in this outcome because if we didn't change, we would lose valuable team members. I was nervous and on edge. It would not be an easy sell to a board steeped in command-and-control management.

My boss made the presentation to a totally quiet room of thirteen board members. After he finished, there was more silence. Then the oldest, both in age and in service on the board, spoke up. He was the executive director of an electric membership organization, a cooperative that provided electricity to rural areas of the state. He had come up through the ranks and was successful and "old school." He had questions. "Who will be in charge, day-to-day? Who will make the tough personnel decisions? Who signs off on vacation time?" It was clear that our proposal was so far from his experience that he couldn't wrap his head around how it would work.

For the next ninety minutes, we heard these same kinds of questions. It was as if we were from Mars and had just landed with this crazy scheme. My heart sank and I felt hopeless. Our team had worked for months to develop a structure built on our values; one that recognized the professional nature of our employees. We had already adopted the changes internally and we were invested in our new vision. We saw a better way, and not being able to move forward would seem like a step back.

Then the chairman of the board, also the vice chancellor at my alma mater, asked me, "How does the staff feel about this approach?"

I think the chairman hoped that my boss was the only one who wanted this change and that I could make it all go away by saying, "The staff likes things now; we don't want to change."

Nervously, I stood up to address him and the board. I had worked closely with them for many years and had earned their trust. Arguing for this new direction could damage that relationship. However, I knew in my heart that it was the right direction for the organization, so I summoned my courage. When I spoke, something came into me and gave me words that were eloquent, heartfelt, and truthful, and they struck a chord with the board members. I have no idea where this voice came from, because I was shy and typically answered their questions in a very succinct fashion—but that day I was an orator, and my speech was a passionate plea. And despite my boss's deer-in-headlights expression, I kept on until I'd made my case.

From the looks on the board members' faces, I didn't think I had convinced anyone to change their mind about our ideas, but I did hope I'd nudged open the door for another possibility.

One of the younger members of the board, an entrepreneur in his early forties, responded to my comments in a way I'll never forget. He said, "Well, Cyndi, everything you just said is motherhood, apple pie, and all that happy horseshit, and I don't think that is the way to run a company."

Motherhood and apple pie? Happy horseshit? His words seemed to make light of my convictions. I felt insulted, and my hopes faded.

"But," he continued, "I do believe the president should choose how he wants to organize the staff and run the business and not the board, and he obviously has support from the staff."

We prevailed in a way I hadn't anticipated, and I was left with three things: a lot of work to do to reorganize the company, curiosity about what had come over me during my speech, and the phrase "motherhood, apple pie, and all that happy horseshit."

I have said those words in my head and out loud over the last twenty-some years. First, they are fun to say. But second, they do sum up what I believe. I believe in motherhood. I believe in nurturing team members, clients, vendors—anyone who is who affiliated with our organization. I believe in apple pie as a symbol of this country and the values of capitalism—not unbridled, greed-based capitalism, but the kind where we can start businesses and be creative, innovative, and rewarded. And I'm a gardener, so give me lots of horseshit because it makes things grow.

While the board member poked fun at me and distilled our grandiose ideas into a catchy phrase that he could easily dismiss, in reality, it became part of my belief system. And it remains a motivator for me as I remember how I fought for and won something because I believed in it.

All these years later, the words encapsulate what is most important to me: being a mom and nurturing my daughter, my team, and my clients; starting my business; and having the confidence to do what I know is right.

Today, bookskeep, the firm I founded, provides accounting services to ecommerce sellers and advises them on profitability. Because of our "motherhood, apple pie, and all that happy horseshit" principles, we have been successful. We've even grown into a seven-figure firm because of the way we care for our team and the way they care for our clients in turn. At a time when everyone orders online and businesses are dealing with automation, we provide a listening ear and a guiding hand to ecommerce entrepreneurs who are too overworked and underprepared to handle all the numbers required to make good decisions.

Ecommerce is growing. Maybe you're considering starting or shifting to an online business. We are in a time of great opportunity for moms or moms-to-be who want the flexibility to both be with their children and keep growing professionally. It has never been easier to become a business owner. I have seen my clients run their companies from all over the world and on just a few hours a day. They have decided what is important to them in life and they have created space for all of it. For many of them, being a mom is priority number one, but committing to that priority does not exclude growing in their professional roles.

I recently received an email from Rebecca, who read my first book, *Profit First for Ecommerce Sellers*. "I had it delivered to Denver to my daughter's house as I help her recover from surgery. I'm eternally grateful for the flexibility ecommerce continues to offer me. Sometimes I feel like I have to pinch myself that this is my life!" Rebecca created a venture that allowed her to continue to prioritize parenting. It means the world to me to receive messages like hers.

My clients are creating their ideal work worlds, and I want that for my team members, too. During the first year of the pandemic, many companies allowed their staff to work from home, and I heard so many complaints from parents who tried to balance their work and parenting responsibilities. Their jobs allowed them to be at home, but also expected them to be at their computers during traditional business hours.

I started bookskeep because I needed flexibility and extra income. I wanted the ability to create my own work schedule and set the expectations for how work would be integrated into my life. I also wanted to be with my daughter, just as my mom had been around for me. I knew from the beginning of my entrepreneurial journey that I had to have the flexibility to work when and where I wanted to work. That is the flexibility I try to create for my team members. Sometimes they work during the day. Sometimes they are with their children during the day and work when their spouses come home and takeover with the children. Sometimes they need to be at school functions or games, so they put in some extra time on the weekend to get their work done. That flexibility is so important to me, and I've made it a part of our culture.

Conventional wisdom says you have to choose between work and your mom role. The expectations of hierarchical and command-and-control style organizations that try to remove the human element from work are leftovers from the industrial age. We now live in an age of information, knowledge workers, and the gig economy. When you tap into someone's knowledge, you want them engaged and all the neurons firing. Neurons don't fire as well when the brain is worried. Worrying about our children—about their well-being and what we're missing—doesn't contribute to peak performance in a knowledge-worker world. As business owners, we can restructure work, and we can do it on our terms, starting with what is best for our family.

I had the privilege of interviewing eleven working moms for this book. All of them have it all. They are not struggling to make it work; they are thriving because they are making it work. When I was growing up in the late 1970s, I heard an Enjoli perfume commercial jingle, based on a popular song, that started like this: "I can bring home the bacon, fry it up in the pan."[1] I assume it was meant to be empowering to women. The message was: You get to do everything. You can have your career, but then go home and continue to take care of your home and family as if it's 1950 and you're June Cleaver from *Leave it to Beaver*. When we "get to do everything," we are not empowered. We are exhausted.

More recently, we've heard from women like Sheryl Sandberg, author of *Lean In,* who again says you can have it all.[2] Susan Adams, in her 2013 *Forbes* article, explains that "*Lean In* is not so much about the balancing act of parenting versus working as it is about the challenges women face in trying to get ahead. Sandberg devotes only three of the book's eleven chapters to work/family balance. The rest are about how women can take charge of their own careers and push forward at a time when gender bias is more alive and well than most of us may want to admit."[3]

In the years between 1978 and the Enjoli commercial, and 2013, when *Lean In* was published, more and more women have entered the work world, and they continue to come home and do the important job of mothering. The stress of doing both well is overwhelming, and if you are a single parent, you shoulder the responsibility alone. In her 2012 article in *The Atlantic*, "Why Women Still Can't Have It All," Anne Marie Slaughter wrote, "It's time to stop fooling ourselves, says a woman who left a position of power: the women who have managed to be both mothers and top professionals are superhuman, rich, or self-employed."[4] I totally agree with her. She explains what I figured out: You can do it all if you are self-employed. Creating your business your way, so it allows you to have the time for both mothering and the income and engagement of work, is entirely possible. And it is exciting, fun, fulfilling, and transformative for you and for all your employees, who may also need a better balance with their family lives.

As a mom, you can have it all—and it's better when you do. When you use your personal values to create the business of your dreams, everyone benefits. Each member of your family grows because you (or both parents) have an opportunity to pursue your dreams and your children observe that example. Your business grows because you attract employees and clients who align with your culture. Finally, *you* grow as you learn to develop and set your direction, manage your priorities, establish boundaries, and solve day-to-day problems for your family and your business.

I wake up every morning excited about the day ahead. I get to watch my daughter make her way in the world. I love that we have the kind of relationship in which she texts and calls with her struggles and with good news. I'm proud that she is confident in her values and her abilities, and I see that the investment I made in her growing up gave her that foundation. I'm also proud when my employees say they are grateful for their job because it allows them time with their kids or grandkids. I feel incredibly blessed that I get to create that opportunity for them, too. When they post pictures of their kids and stories of their exploits, it makes me just as happy as I feel when we get glowing client testimonials. Giving women the opportunity to become fully themselves, and experience the joy of work and family, is really what it's all about for me.

I wrote this book to help you have it all. Not to help you *do* it all, but to have the whole life you want, when you want it. I'm a living example of what is possible, and so are the women whose stories I've shared with you in this book. In these pages, you'll find from-the-trenches wisdom, exercises that will help you get clarity and reclaim what matters to you, and tools I created just for you to help you ensure that you grow a healthy venture. Whether you're just starting out or are a seasoned entrepreneur and looking for better balance, this book will help you design a business that supports you and your family.

I say, let's go for motherhood, apple pie, and happy horseshit! Let's get started so you can create your life, your way!

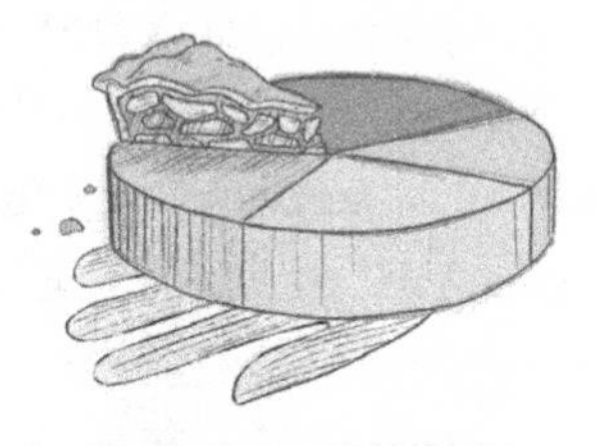

CHAPTER 1

YOU CAN DO THIS!

DURING A TYPICAL MONDAY MORNING taxi ride in late 1997, I asked a question that would change our lives forever: Is this the right time to start a family?

In the last year that I worked my corporate job, every week started off the same way. Monday morning was a flurry of activity: packing for the week, tidying the house, checking in at the office, and calling for a taxi to take us to the airport. My husband Dave and I would typically catch early morning flights to our work destinations for the week.

As we left our suburban neighborhood on this particular Monday, we got an update on expected travel time from the taxi driver and his assurance that we'd make our flights. Finally still for a few moments, we looked out the car windows at the growing neighborhoods we passed.

"Cary is getting fifteen new residents a day," the taxi driver told us. Dave and I loved the North Carolina town and had called it home for fifteen years. It was a great place to live, even though the roads weren't keeping up with the traffic.

During the rest of the quiet twenty-minute ride, Dave and I talked about our plans. We both had great jobs. I had been at Advanced Energy for more than ten years and had grown in my responsibilities. After years of managing administration in the areas of accounting, contracts, human resources, etc., I was now serving as Vice President of Business Development. Dave had finished his MBA at Duke University and was consulting for KPMG and traveling to help develop activity-based costing systems for heavy manufacturing clients all over the East Coast. We could have kept these jobs and grown in these businesses. Yet Dave itched to have his turn at running a manufacturing facility. He had worked in engineering and supervisory roles and was now consulting with financial leaders. He could see how it all came together and wanted the chance to make it work under his direction. As we talked about this possibility, it became clear that his next job would require us to move.

While we headed toward to the freeway, the well-maintained neighborhoods of Cary formed the backdrop for our conversation.

Dave asked, "Is it the right time to consider changing jobs for both of us?"

I was not really keen on getting another job; I was working at my dream job. My entire career had been with the same company. I had started as a receptionist and worked my way through the ranks to a position on the leadership team. I felt accomplished, as I'd also earned my bachelor's degree in economics while working full-time. I was fulfilled and on-purpose. No job could be better than what I already had.

And yet I worried that, as a woman in my mid-thirties, my window to have a child had started to close. If I didn't have children, would I miss out on some of the richness of life?

That's when I asked the question that would change the trajectory of our lives: "How about you get a new job and we try to get pregnant, and I won't work until the baby goes to school?"

Where did those words come from? Was I really ready to consider this possibility?

Dave thought for a minute; he always pauses to choose just the right words. He said, "If that's what you want, let's do it. I can see that working."

I started running through the impact of such a decision. We'd be living without my income for a few years, and we enjoyed our comfortable lifestyle. It allowed us to have nice furniture and new cars, and travel whenever we had the time off. Two high-level positions with great compensation allowed us to afford this life. Could we handle the adjustment to our standard of living? What about the cost of raising a child? How would we afford that if I didn't work? I knew from a financial perspective that it would be a challenge. I also knew that I wanted to be at home, not work during those early years. I had this ideal childhood in my mind that I wanted to create, and I couldn't see work as part of that picture.

In my heart, I was also concerned about working a demanding job and taking care of a baby. I was sure that I would be heartbroken to leave my child and stressed out if I tried to juggle work responsibilities when I wanted to be with her.

I recalled a friend and coworker calling me in total panic mode one morning. She had taken her child to daycare on her way to the office as usual, but as she got out of the car, she accidentally locked the door with the keys inside, the car running, and her baby in the car seat. It was cold outside and she was worried that her car would run out of gas before she could get in and her baby would get cold. She tried to hold it all together, and then her baby started to cry. It was tears for all of us. Luckily, the police came and my friend was in her car in no time.

Experiences like this convinced me that I would feel scattered and overwhelmed trying to work and take care of a little one. I wanted to be home with my child.

Dave said, "If I get a good plant manager's job, maybe I could make enough for you to stay at home with our baby?"

Talking about starting a family on our own terms gave us a sense of possibility.

Now on the freeway and stuck in traffic, our plan started to take shape. Dave had been contacted by a headhunter, who mentioned a job in the Midwest. We knew that we would have to leave our family and our friends, but the lower cost of living in rural Missouri—along with a nice bump in salary for Dave—made it worth considering as part of this new "family plan."

By the time we arrived at the airport, we had made the huge decision to start down this path. Dave would move forward with the job interview, and I would research the actual cost of living for the new location and contact our realtor to determine what the housing market looked like for the possible sale of our home.

Once we started to take these small steps, the path unfolded before us. In a few short months, we resigned from our jobs, sold our home in North Carolina, and started a new life in Missouri.

Our daughter was nine when I decided to start my business. We needed a little extra money, and I missed my identity as a professional person. I missed work. Now, though, I could create a business built around my personal values. For me, that meant putting our daughter first.

Deciding how to fit a new child into your routines, and how to handle the work and the new role of mothering, is one part planning and three hundred parts emotion. You may be wondering how you can possibly manage your corporate career, which demands so much time, energy, and focus, and be the mother you desire to be for your child. Maybe you are home with your baby, considering how you will handle the logistical demands once your maternity leave is over and childcare, work, and a commute are everyday realities. Maybe you are dreading the idea of leaving your child behind and can feel that coming heartbreak. Possibly, you are experiencing the greatest love of your life, yet feel detached from a part of you that was doing work you were passionate about, or feel disconnected from your purpose, disengaged from achieving your goals, or isolated from the people in your network. Perhaps this little bundle of joy that has stolen your heart is causing you to rethink your goals. Maybe going to the office and working for someone else isn't appealing anymore, especially now that you need more flexibility. Or is the idea you've always thought about for a business screaming in your ear?

These are all-consuming thoughts, and they keep you up at night. You worry because you will have to go back to work soon and that entails heartache and logistical stress, or you worry because you are not planning to go back to work right away and being at home full-time is causing you to feel like you don't really know who you are anymore.

As moms who also hold down jobs or run businesses, we are excellent problem-solvers. Look: You already found a book to help you. You have taken the first step toward creating a work and home life that is driven by your personal values and heartfelt desires.

The concerns you have and the reasons behind them may differ, and so will the solutions. Rest assured, there are options, and you are not stuck. Women have been solving this issue for years, and our creativity and resourcefulness always see us through. Let's start by reframing the most fundamental issue around separating our business and personal lives and get in touch with what you really want.

BUSINESS IS PERSONAL

We've all been on the receiving end of bad news at work. Maybe you didn't get a promotion or a raise, or your project wasn't funded. Whatever the news, we often hear the same phrase: "This isn't personal; it's just business." Our managers believe or pretend that disappointing news is somehow less disappointing if it's just part of the job, that this news won't impact you emotionally because it's not personal.

When I was in college, my boss at my first office job told me not to mix my work life with my personal life. "Keep work friends at work," he said, and don't socialize together outside of the office. In some organizations, "hanging out" with lower-level employees is simply not allowed because it can interfere with your judgment; yet you spend most of your waking hours with these work buddies. When you have a bad day on the job, you share this with your partner at home. When things are a mess at home, you seek advice from trusted friends at work. How do you leave friendships with colleagues in the parking lot when you head home and leave the home issues in the driveway when you head to the office?

"It's not personal, it's business" and other popular adages have been a part of our business culture for so long, we accept them without question. We accept their validity without understanding where they come from and if they are relevant today.

As you embark on this journey, I invite you to suspend your beliefs and look at this from a different perspective. In one of my favorite books, *The Art of Possibility*, authors Benjamin and Rosamund Zander help us realize "it's all invented."[5] Our perception of reality—how we frame the issues—allows us to create the solutions to our challenges. In fact, the story behind the "Nothing personal, it's just business" quote can be viewed as an argument against the message itself. The phrase was coined in the early 1900s by an accountant, Otto "Abbadabba" Berman. Otto had the ability to figure complex mathematical equations in a matter of seconds without the use of paper or pen. He put this talent to use as an accountant and advisor for gangster and mafia boss Dutch Schultz. Otto died in 1935 at the hands of assassins hired by Lucky Luciano.[6] His business dealings cost him his life; you don't get much more personal than that. Ironically, his story disproves the adage he was famous for and supports the tenet that business is personal.

As a mom and a business owner, I can tell you: It's *all* personal. The reason I started my business, the reason I hire people, the reason I work in my industry, the reason I don't work with some clients—these are all personal decisions. Yes, my approach impacts my business, but I make these decisions with the help of other team members, and it's all about what we want as people. "Take care of people and the business will take care of itself" is one of my personal principles.

This personal principle is unconventional. It's not how most businesses operate. We saw that in big, bold numbers during the middle of the pandemic when, in September of 2020, 865,000 women left the workforce because school was starting and "someone" had to stay home to care for and try to assist with teaching their children.[7] Rather than businesses investing in and supporting women and families, women quit their jobs.

As a woman contemplating owning a business while also mothering, this idea that we must separate our business and personal worlds—and behave in different ways in each world—may be at such odds with your vision of living with integrity in all areas that entrepreneurship does not look like a reasonable option for you. This premise of separate worlds and separate "personalities" lies at the core of some of those questions that keep you up at night.

There are so many considerations in both mothering and creating a business. You may be questioning if you can do it all. You can. You may be wondering how you can keep parenthood and work separated. You can't. In fact, your superpower will shine as you learn to accept the overlap and make a life that works for you and your family. Your business will be personal to you, and that is what will make it great.

The truth is, the lines between business and our personal lives are indistinct. In fact, they not really lines at all. They are more like blurry, curvy, messy smudges that are impossible to separate. Pretending you can separate these paths creates unrealistic expectations that can leave you feeling depleted and frustrated. Learning to integrate your business and personal lives will make both richer and enrich the people in both circles. I'm writing this on November 1, and last night I had so much fun seeing the pictures of my team members' children dressed up for Halloween. I'm so glad that we all can share in that bit of fun. Why would I ever want to keep that kind of communication out of the office? It is a great way for us to connect and share about important parts of our lives.

WHAT'S IN THE WAY CAN BE THE WAY

HERE IS ANOTHER WAY TO reframe the issue: What is in your way is quite possibly the way forward. I recently attended a workshop given by a phenomenal coach, Andrea Lee. She helped us understand how to progress with a project by asking us about our fears and what would stop us from moving forward.

After probing this question with several participants, she said, "What's in the way can be the way."

Andrea's quiet delivery of this simple sentence was so understated that it almost slipped by me. But when I processed it, whoa! It was like opening the door to a portal that transported me to another world—a world where, for the first time, I understood that what had been in the way my entire life had actually become the way. Education was that thing. There was always something I had to learn to be able to accomplish my next goal. Working on my degree part-time while I worked full-time, taking courses so I could help my daughter with homeschool—the actual learning I had to do set me up to value education. Today, in my personal and business life, learning and educating are the ways I differentiate myself and add value. I teach "Know Your Numbers" webinars for clients. I wrote a book to help our clients understand their finances. We don't just do the books for our clients, we want them to understand them, and education is a key part of our service. The fulfillment of being both a mom and a business owner, and getting to live out my purpose of educating my daughter, employees, clients, and readers, was all possible and intensified once I gave myself the sacred space to consider what was really important to me and how to work with what was in the way.

What's in the way of your being a great mother and starting a business? Since we have reframed our understanding of business and know that it is and will continue to be personal, let's look at each of these obstacles and consider our fears and the most likely results. We will temper these fears with reality and not get caught up in expecting perfection in all areas every day.

- I am worried that when I'm working, my child will feel ignored or I will miss some important milestones.

  This will probably happen on occasion, but you'll manage and set schedules that work and minimize this occurrence.

- I am afraid that I will be overwhelmed, trying to do it all.

This will happen. Before I had a child, I felt overwhelmed at work some days. After I had a child, I felt overwhelmed at home. This feeling is part of the human experience, and you learn to set boundaries as you establish your priorities.

- I am concerned that my work will suffer if I am distracted with caring for my child at home.

  Your work may suffer on occasion but, as a business owner, you will focus on the important things and rely on support from both your professional and personal support networks.

- I am afraid that I'm not organized enough, creative enough, etc. (You fill-in-the-blank enough.)

  You are always enough! You will figure it out and get the support you need.

- I am concerned that my business idea may not work, and I'll have taken time away from my child and regret it. Or maybe it will be wildly successful, and I'll have to take more time away from my child. I am also afraid that if I don't follow my vision to create a business, I'll regret it.

  There is no way to tell the future. And there is no shame in failing; it is really just learning. Your children will learn so much from you pursuing your dreams, and so will you.

- My partner, spouse, family, friends, etc. (you fill in the blank) have definite ideas that may get in my way.

It's guaranteed that they have ideas, so talk with them and try out the ideas if they make sense to you. Listen and learn and start to set and manage their expectations. The real caution, though, is for you to remember that you get to make the decision, not them. Give yourself the time and space to determine what you want.

- I believe that my business and personal lives must be separate.

  There are so many cultural norms that shape our beliefs. Are there societal or cultural obstacles in your way? Consider them, but realize that they may not have any validity in our world today. If they don't help you, then move in the directions of your dreams.

This is a very personal choice, and I respect those who don't follow the same path that I chose. I do suggest that if you find yourself asking those questions, pay attention and examine them. Be deliberate about creating your life; don't get swept up in the demands of a job and family and ignore what you really want. This book is all about moving forward once you have made the choice to have kids, when you know you desire to create a life that allows you to spend time with them on your terms and stay engaged in a professional or business endeavor.

In the pages to come, we will explore these concerns as we learn from other moms who work or run a business. There is no one-size-fits-all answer here. We don't need to reinvent the wheel, either. Learning what worked for these moms—and what didn't—will help you explore your options. The key is to consider what makes sense for you and your family and know that it may change over time, as your world changes.

YOU CAN HAVE IT ALL

THERE WILL ALWAYS BE CHALLENGES. They will be different for you than for anyone else. Your business ideas are different, your children will be different, your technological needs will be different, and your support network will be different. No matter your challenges, there are ways to make it work and the key to uncovering those ways lies within you. You can have children and have a business, and when you create the space to uncover your desires, as you will learn to do in the next chapter, you can determine how your life will work.

If you are motivated to create both roles in your life, then you will find a way. While it won't be easy, it will be fulfilling. As I said earlier, as entrepreneurs and moms, we're great problem-solvers. You will start to see each challenge as something else to overcome. You will get so good at overcoming that those mountains really do become molehills, just steps in your journey.

I'm leaving all the angst and emotion and crying I experienced on my own journey out of this chapter. As you will read in the stories throughout this book, though, there is usually plenty of that. If you are a mom without a business, there will be plenty of that. If you are a business owner and not a parent, there will be plenty of that. And weirdly—in a non-math way—when you put them together, they don't actually add up. You see, the skills, discernment, and confidence you gain from doing both actually make doing each a little easier.

When you get in touch with your dreams, you live with a little more ease and a lot more grace.

The path I've laid out for you in this book will help you have it all, on your own terms. In the first part of the book, you'll set up your world to create a life based on your personal values. Then I'll walk you through some of the strategies I used to build a business that supported my life. You'll find exercises at the end of each chapter that encourage you to get in touch with your unique desires and offering. These exercises will prompt you to do deep work as you are called:

- To spend time reflecting and being brutally honest about what is important to you;
- To let go of expectations that society, your family, and even you may have that aren't aligned with your goals; and
- To develop a plan and get started. The details will get sorted along the way, just as they did for me and all the other moms in this book.

Once I started my business, I gained perspective, confidence, and ease. All aspects of my world seemed to be in better harmony. It is a struggle to achieve worklife integration, but it is so worth it. Yes, you can have it all—on your terms. And you know what? It's better when you *do* have it all. Your family will be happier. Your team will be happier. Your clients will be happier. And most importantly, *you* will be happier.

There is never enough time, and yet I know that when you're up all night and unsure when you'll get to shower again, the time seems to drag. (Everyone who has lived through it will tell you the same thing, and I expect you have heard it before.)

The ease for me began to develop as I recognized that I had wanted a child without really understanding the full impact it would have on me. I didn't anticipate the loss of the part of my identity that was tied up in my work role. Ignoring that aspect of who I was made the day-to-day so much harder. Exploring and giving full credence to what you want for yourself makes your work as a mother so much more rewarding because you come from a place of wholeness instead of a place of lack.

To help you navigate this time and all the questions, I've gathered the most significant lessons and best tips and tricks I've learned along the way to share with you in these pages. I will also share some best experiences from other moms and entrepreneurs to help you realize that you can do it too—and you *will* do it your own way.

And I want to hear from you, too. I want to learn what business you are considering, what your current family status is, and what concerns may be holding you back. Send me an email at ct@cyndithomason.com. I will write you back and give you my honest thoughts about your situation. I will invite you into my community, where we can collectively support each other.

WHAT IS IN YOUR WAY *IS* THE WAY

Suggested Time to Complete: Twenty minutes.

When you complete this exercise, you will have moved your fears and worries about starting a business out of your head and onto paper. You will be able to state them in specific and solvable terms.

⊗ **IF YOU SKIP THIS EXERCISE,** you commit an act of self-sabotage. Instead of identifying and solving your fears and challenges, you will dwell on them. As a result, you will hold yourself back from making progress toward the life you want.

Take a minute to jot down your concerns. What worries you about starting a business? About parenting? What are your fears about trying to do both?

Permit yourself the freedom to get this out of your head and down on paper. You aren't trying to solve the challenges in this exercise; you are just documenting them. As you do, try to state your concerns in precise terms and to avoid "always" and "never" statements. If you think of your challenges in those terms, which are unrealistic, you give them too much power.

TOO BROAD	SPECIFIC (AND SOLVABLE!)
If I start a business, I will never spend enough time with my kids.	I am worried I will be so busy that I'll need after-school care for my kids; I want to have afternoons and evenings with my family. I am afraid I won't be there for bedtime each night. I am worried I won't be able to volunteer in the classroom.

As you work through this book, you will read examples and get ideas from other mom entrepreneurs. And you will find that often, the problem they faced *became the solution*. For example, Julie is a periodontist who has her whole practice operating on a 3:00 p.m. stop time so she can be with her daughter in the afternoons. Her employees (many of whom are also parents) love it, and her clients appreciate the early start times. So, as you read this book, permit yourself to think differently. You might just figure out how something that was in the way becomes the way.

⌛ **FAST FIVE:** If you are short on time, write down just *one* specific challenge or fear on a sticky note or small slip of paper. Tuck it between these pages and keep reading. When you find a solution, come back to this page, remove the note, and destroy it. You're going to bust through those challenges!

PROGRESS NUGGET: *Nearly one in four Americans won't read a book at all this year. In picking up this book, working through these exercises, and walking the path of entrepreneurship, you're doing something extraordinary—but it can sometimes feel like a lonely path. Find support and community with a like-minded group of mom entrepreneurs at ApplePieMoms.com or the QR Code below:*

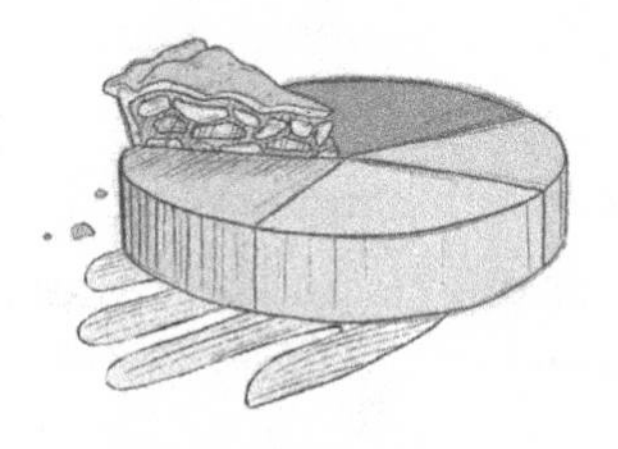

CHAPTER 2

SACRED SPACE IS THE BIRTHPLACE OF YOUR DREAMS

When we are caught up in the busy-ness of everyday life, it can be a challenge to allow possibility and inspiration to work their magic. We answer all the questions for our families and employees. We plan meals and transportation and meetings and marketing campaigns. We are in a constant state of giving. All of this takes a toll. I know we like it, though. It is an ego trip to have all the answers and make the well-oiled machines of work and family life hum thanks to our ability to plan and improvise and organize. It is all very fulfilling until it isn't.

There comes a time when we no longer feel appreciated or even care about making that next decision. We just want someone else to take over for the day. At this point—really, before we ever reach this point—we need guidance to help us find our way.

In the past, no matter our individual circumstances or cultures, we have had myths and legends to help us understand the events of our lives. These myths pointed to explanations in the external world, explanations for the changes in our bodies as we grew up, had children, grew old, and passed away. The myths also helped us understand our roles in society. In *The Power of Myth*, Joseph Campbell states, "The stages of human development are the same today as they were in ancient times. As a child, you are brought up in a world of discipline, of obedience, and you are dependent on others. All this has to be transcended when you come to maturity, so that you can live not in dependency but with self-responsible authority."[8] Today though, we as women and as mothers have much more opportunity. We lack myths and legends to help us understand the transitions and import of many of life's journeys. For example, when a woman returns to work after maternity leave, it is a stressful, unsettling time. I don't know of any business that recognizes this milestone. We celebrate the birth with a baby shower and gifts, but what about the return to the workplace and the daily separation from the child? We need a ceremony to mark this occasion. With so many amazing technological advances, we as a society are changing so fast that our myths of old can't keep up. For many of us, the roles our mothers played have no bearing on what we may choose for ourselves. Our mothers faced much more limiting choices than we have today. While many cultures now afford more opportunity for women and moms in the professional realm, the guidance from our heritage simply doesn't relate.

In the absence of myths to guide our way, where do we turn?

My experience was to turn inward, to really come to understand what was and is important to me. In *The Power of Myth*, Campbell also discusses the importance of finding your "bliss station." He recommends that we dedicate an hour a day to something that causes us to lose track of the ever-growing to-do list, financial worries, and other expectations and anxieties.[9] I took his advice to heart. I spend that hour—and more—gardening, but the bliss station will be unique for each of us and is likely to change over the years. I call the bliss station, and the resulting state of being, "Sacred Space."

It may seem odd that, in a book about how to work and parent on your terms, I am asking you to find time for a hobby—but it is the start of the process. When you allow yourself the time to experience whatever brings you joy, you open a Sacred Space within yourself that you can cultivate and grow as a place of knowing. In this place, you can create, rejuvenate, and get in touch with what you find important in life. In your Sacred Space, you will connect to what you really want and who you really are. You will remember how life and work were modeled for you and consider how much of that you want to carry forward into your own life. You will start to design a path that makes sense for you and your family.

Motherhood is a heroic act and it requires sacrifice, just like the hero stories told in many of the cultural myths of the past. In *The Power of Myth*, Joseph Campbell writes that "Giving birth is definitely a heroic deed, in that it is the giving over of oneself to the life of another. That's a big change…"[10] We give up so much to care for our children. Motherhood takes a toll. Staying in touch with your Sacred Space puts the sacrifice into perspective and ensures that you can continue to give. By allowing yourself this time each day, you will be able to maintain your identity and stay true to yourself during these years when you give so much to your family.

WHAT HAPPENS IN SACRED SPACE?

SACRED SPACE ENCOMPASSES MULTIPLE DIMENSIONS. It's your quiet time to think. It's the physical space where you don't work on mentally demanding business or personal tasks. It's the internal awareness of what makes you whole, the connection to your universal truth, your spiritual guides, God. It's losing yourself in exercise or a hobby that creates a connection to flow. When you disconnect from the daily busy-ness, you connect to your core identity. While the word "sacred" has religious definitions that may apply to your world view, it also is defined as something that is treated with great respect. Either or both may apply for you.

When I'm in my garden, I lose myself. And, as I type this, I realize that what I really mean is I *find* myself. I lose the day-to-day noise and expectations and find a closer connection to my core. Getting my hands dirty, hearing the bees and hummingbirds whiz by, pulling weeds, deadheading spent flower blooms, cultivating the soil, and laying down mulch causes me to totally disconnect from my mentally demanding world. If I'm puzzling over something at work, it is set aside. If I'm concerned about a family matter, it takes a backseat. The thoughts may come into my awareness, but they pass on by because I give them no attention. When my time in the garden is done, I clean and put away my tools. I wash up and, if I take a moment to notice, I realize that I'm relaxed. I'm connected to something bigger than myself—or maybe it's deep inside me, beyond the control of my ego.

When I put my attention back on business or personal matters after time in my Sacred Space, I have a new perspective.

There is a knowing, an undercurrent of faith that the proper course, the answer to a prayer will arise at the right moment. With this knowing, the need to plan and control steps aside just long enough for other possibilities to step forward. When those new ideas arise, they come from an inspired place. They aren't forced; they are allowed. As they unfold, they shine in ways that forced solutions never can. Forced solutions show all the dings and divots from being hammered into place. They are dull and exhausting. A solution arising from my Sacred Space reflects the light because it came from light.

In this book, you will find many practical thought exercises to help you create the life you want. I encourage you to use your Sacred Space to work through these exercises. *Lose yourself to find yourself.*

One way to do this is to designate a journaling practice in which you write about your ideas and concerns so you can look at them dispassionately. Often, getting the emotions on paper shows you the fears that are in the way. Once you can see those fears in writing, you can start to investigate them more deeply. You can give yourself space to put them aside, gain perspective, and allow ideas to surface that will help you resolve or even dismiss the original idea or problem.

Some moms prefer the opportunity to talk through their ideas or challenges with other moms. For them, lunch with a friend or group of friends in their support network can help them connect to their Sacred Space. I often joke that I don't know what I'm thinking until it comes out of my mouth. Talking about the issue allows me to clarify my thinking. Saying something out loud can make me realize that, for example, my fear is irrational or can be easily addressed. Even if it is a real factor to overcome, getting support from others makes the struggle less lonely and less overwhelming.

You may already have a hobby or sport that allows you to get into "the zone" and want to recommit to it. Perhaps you like to spend time in prayer or meditation. The point is to find your way, your why, using the methods that work best for you. Then ensure that you make time in your week to keep that connection. Realize that the hobby or sport, the physical space, the act of journaling or talking to moms, or the prayer or meditation is a fundamental requirement for you to stay true to the Sacred Space in your heart. All the messiness that comes with life, family, and business will make sense and feel rewarding if you operate from that centered Sacred Space.

TIME TO THINK

LAURA FOUND HER SOLUTION THROUGH her Sacred Space. A professional colleague of mine, Laura, lives in Australia and has a virtual accounting firm called Adroit Business Solutions. She started her business prior to becoming a mom because she wanted to travel. Laura had the luxury of figuring out how to work remotely before adding her first son, Eitan, into the mix. She was process-oriented and had her systems dialed in. However, she was actively performing almost all the work. When she got pregnant with Eitan, she realized things would have to be different because her priorities were going to be different. She knew that her time away during maternity leave was going to impact her ability to serve her clients. Laura jumped into action.

When I interviewed her for this book, she told me, "I was worried about how I could be a really good mother and keep the business going because the business was still very dependent on me. I worked by myself for many, many years before I decided that I wanted a team. At this stage, I had one team member and she was good, but she couldn't run the business."

Laura made the decision to continue working as she managed childcare for her newborn even though it would be hard. She determined first that she needed a routine. Wisely, Laura realized that she must create Sacred Space as part of that routine.

Laura explained, "I created a routine that gave me time to think and reflect. I would get up, get Eitan fed and ready to go either on my back or into a pram, and we'd walk for ages. That gave me time and space with my thoughts. He was quiet. I came to terms with the fact that I didn't feel good, and I couldn't understand why. There wasn't anything really wrong, but still, I struggled."

Because the business was still dependent on her and she wanted to be with her child as long as possible, she had to get creative. "I knew that I didn't want to send my child to daycare until he was nine months old, at the minimum. Obviously, I was striving for twelve months or longer, but I knew that realistically, the business was still quite dependent on me. I came to terms with the idea that I might go back sooner, but I wasn't going to compromise and go back after three weeks, six weeks, three months, or whatever."

Laura found a solution: babywearing. Laura is a teacher at heart, and she always wants to help others. Once she found a solution, she didn't put her head down and work, she created a new opportunity for adult interaction and became the president of a babywearing group.

"I wore my son literally everywhere; when I worked, when I walked, everything. It saved my sanity when I had to work when I didn't necessarily want to work. Luckily, he was a kid that was very comfortable in the wrap. And even though I found something that allowed me to work, I was really scared, and I felt guilty, because I couldn't see how I could be a good mother at the same time.

"I struggled because I realized that I was really unhappy as a full-time mother. There is this picture painted that it's the most miraculous and amazing time, and it is. They grow up so quickly and the bond is so important and all of that; and I agree with all those things. Yet I don't think all our time has to be spent as moms." Laura reached the same conclusion that I had reached. We can do it all if we do it on our own terms, listen to our inner voice rather than society, and then let that voice guide us as we create the environment we need in both our family and work lives.

Laura's time for reflection revealed what she needed. "I knew I thrived when I was challenging my brain. You hear a lot of people saying you need to have self-care. For me, self-care was getting out and having interesting and inspiring conversations and challenging my brain, which I did not get as a stay-at-home mother. And one of the things that got me through the times when it felt really hard was a routine. My routine was a walk and then coffee, then activities with my child, because I could have interactions with other people as well. Then it would be nap time and I could get some work done. That was probably my favorite time of the day—not because I was away from my child, but because I got that stimulation. And that's how I realized what was happening for me."

Laura needed time to think, and she created that Sacred Space while walking with her baby. She realized that walks and naps gave her time to think more deeply, and processing her thoughts gave her the chance to gain self-knowledge and put her analytical skills to work. Once she understood the analysis, she knew what to do to make the business and mothering work together.

MOTHERING BASED ON HOW WE WERE MOTHERED

When you are in Sacred Space, you make room for new insights. In some cases, these are insights about your past that will help you design your future. So often, we are on autopilot, making decisions about work or parenting without thinking the about the why behind them. Losing yourself for an hour or so a day helps you gain awareness and make decisions based on that awareness.

When I was a little girl, the sound of the sewing machine from the great room next to my bedroom was a constant whirr. I always knew that my mom was just a few steps away. I heard the whirr in the afternoons while I worked on my homework. That sound was the background to every TV show in the evening. It was the sound I went to sleep to and often the first sound I heard when waking up. The sound was comforting. I knew my mom was creating something cool. New clothes for me, a wedding dress for my cousin, new curtains for our house, a dress for my aunt. I could see her creativity shine. She glowed with a special light and joy while creating clothing.

Growing up, I didn't really understand the motivation behind my mom's sewing projects. In fact, I didn't even think about it. Now, many years later, it's clear that at least one reason she sewed was to help our family financially. We were farmers, and while I never wanted for anything that I needed, it wasn't an easy life and the money tended to come in big chunks a few times a year, like at wheat harvest or when the calves sold. Whether it was making clothes for growing kids to save on expenses or bringing in extra money from selling clothing, sewing projects helped my mom stretch the dollars.

Sewing was a way to work from home, for her to be close to me and my brother and available to drive equipment to a field or help with the cattle and add to the family income. I understand this completely now and realize that it profoundly influenced my life and how I chose to raise my daughter. Later, it gave me the confidence to start my business to build in flexibility, grow our income, and engage with adults rather than return to a job as a corporate employee or continue as a stay-at-home mom.

Our concept of being a mom is rooted in our experience of being mothered. There are assumptions that you may not realize are in your awareness. As a mom, what are you trying to create? And why? Are you afraid you can't recreate your idyllic childhood, or are you afraid you'll recreate the difficult childhood you experienced?

I wanted to recreate my childhood experience for my daughter. My friend AJ wanted to create a very different experience from her own for her son.

When I interviewed AJ for this book, she told me she doesn't remember her parents married. She was three years old when they divorced. Her mom was pursuing her PhD in ancient history, and AJ tagged along to the university.

"It was me and Mom against the world," she said.

They were very close, and that closeness increased when they went to Egypt for an archaeological dig as part of her mom's PhD requirements. Unfortunately, AJ got sick, and her mother flew back with her to Minnesota to get treatment. A few weeks later, her mom returned to Egypt, leaving AJ with her dad.

AJ's grandmother came to live with her and her dad to help out. She was the mother of eleven children, and she knew how to make things cozy and right for a child. She met the bus, had snacks ready, and ensured that the meals were made and laundry was done. AJ settled into a life where she was the center of the family even though her dad worked in his office five and a half days a week as a CPA and brought work home in the evening. The sound of the adding machine was typical after dinner during tax season.

After about a year, AJ's mom returned and started her own business with an invention that improved the typesetting process. The venture demanded much of her time, and AJ was once again pushed down the priority list. Once she began attending school, her mom was late picking her up every day. AJ was always the last to leave. As the school emptied, she would sit in the office with a frustrated staff member, waiting on her mom. This being the norm, not the exception, it became apparent to AJ that her parents were work-centric and not child-centric, even though she also knew that she was loved unconditionally.

As AJ developed friendships in school, she found a way to avoid the last-one-to-leave situation. Her best friend, Stacie, invited her to come to her home in the afternoons. There, AJ saw a different family dynamic. She saw Stacie's mom—also an entrepreneur, an antique shop owner—take time in the shop in the afternoons to spend with the girls. AJ would have a lot of sleepovers with Stacie. As she became integrated in their family life, AJ said, "Stacie's mom became my second mom."

When AJ was a fifteen-year-old freshman in high school, the news came that her school would close after that academic year. She had to apply and get accepted into a new school in the city. One afternoon, her dad arrived to pick her up. This was unusual, and he explained that her mom needed to get away and had left town. Her business was causing a lot of stress. For the foreseeable future, AJ would live with her dad. This created some logistical issues because her dad lived an hour and a half from her school. After a while, three hours in the car every day took a toll on both of them.

In addition, once again, AJ had been abandoned by her mom and was dealing with those difficult emotions at a time when she was developing her identity. She already knew she would do things differently if she were the mother. In fact, she took matters into her own hands and found a school close to her dad's home. She applied, wrote the essay, and completed the interview process before her mom returned.

"I wanted stability," she told me. "So I created it for myself."

AJ's collective childhood experiences set her intention for when she was a mom. She knew her child would be the center of her world and that her child would feel that. She would not allow her child to feel like they were less than top priority. She had seen how her grandmother and Stacie's mom had made children a priority, and she had felt how a sense of importance to a parent was crucial. As a result, when she had her son, she made different choices. She chose to build her work life in such a way that she could be with him as much as possible, to create a child-centric family.

Your backstory may be very different from mine or AJ's, but it's what motivates you that matters. Whatever it is in your background that drives you, it will help you develop your set of values going forward. You are striving to achieve something with your life. You want to create your future as well as set something in motion for your child. You may be trying to reconcile your experience or recreate it. It is my hope that you will do this consciously, honoring the past in consideration of your future. And you can do that in Sacred Space.

FINDING YOUR SACRED SPACE

Suggested Time to Complete: Thirty minutes.

When you complete this exercise, you will be in touch with your personal Sacred Space. Understanding and adeptly accessing this space will allow you to find answers to the deep questions that arise as you make parenting decisions and begin to form your business.

If you skip this exercise, you will make this process harder on yourself. Sacred Space is an important concept that will recur throughout this book and is vital for your creation of a life and a business you love. If you don't understand your Sacred Space, you may be swimming upstream for the entire process. Leave the swimming upstream to the salmon (who, by the way, don't survive the process)!

If you are feeling a little confused about what Sacred Space is, that's totally okay! It looks different for everyone, and everyone arrives at theirs differently. You almost certainly have a Sacred Space; this exercise will help you better identify it, so you can visit it—and reap the benefits—more frequently.

In your Sacred Space, you can uncover your truths, work past the limiting beliefs that are holding you back and tap into the creativity that will propel you in the direction you most desire. Being in your Sacred Space is *not* about purposefully concentrating and trying to solve a problem. It is about losing the problem so that answers can come to you more readily.

At first, you may not recognize that you *are* in your Sacred Space until you suddenly find clarity on an issue you have been struggling with. If you've ever gone for a jog or a hike and come back feeling clear and confident about something, you've found Sacred Space.

You may already understand your Sacred Space and how you can get "there." Or you may not. In either case, go through this exercise so you can claim it as your own.

1. **Define "sacred" for you.** While the term may conjure up images of prayer or meditation, these ideas should not limit you. Think about times in your life when you felt clarity and surety in your thoughts and your state of flow (maybe one of them brought you to this book!). Note the environment you were in at the time and what you were doing—and not doing.
2. **Choose a physical space (or two) or activity.** You may find Sacred Space while being still and quiet in a favorite place. Or you may find it when you are active

and separating your higher thinking from the part of your brain that's moving one foot in front of the other on a run, keeping you balanced in downward dog, or digging a new garden bed.

3. **Choose a time.** Choose a time when you can be with your thoughts without distraction. The bench in your yard near the fragrant roses may be a place where you can enter your Sacred Space when you're alone, but if the kids are jumping on the trampoline fifteen feet away, it will be challenging to be alone with your thoughts. Going for a run while pushing a stroller and doling out snacks won't clear your head as a solo run will. Pick a time just for you; this may be before your family gets up in the morning, after they are in bed at night, during school hours, or at some other time when you are with only yourself.
4. **Choose your talisman.** It would be great to have a truly magical object that could instantly transport you to your sacred space (and maybe fold the laundry and vacuum, too). If only such a thing existed. But you can have special objects and rituals that you associate only with your Sacred Space, like your journal, making loose-leaf tea in your favorite teapot, lacing up your running shoes, or pulling on your garden gloves.
5. **Develop your ritual.** Rituals help orient our minds and define the state we are about to enter. Incorporate the physical space, time, and talisman you've already identified into a ritual or script that will be a gateway into your Sacred Space. It might look like something like this:

> *At 8:45 a.m., I get home from dropping the kids off at school (TIME). Before the day gets too warm (TIME), I change into my gardening clothes (RITUAL) and get my good gloves and my favorite garden tools (TALISMAN). I head out to the garden (PLACE) and start turning over the beds that are due for winter crops and then continue on from there.*

If you're still stuck on where your Sacred Space is and how to enter it, here are some examples of what works for the business-owner moms featured in this book:

- Gardening
- Jogging
- Yoga
- Journaling
- Sewing
- Kintsugi pottery-mending
- Painting

⧗ **Fast Five:** Sacred Space is vital to your journey in starting a business or running a thriving business. If you can't devote twenty to thirty minutes to the exercise above and want to keep on reading, take five minutes and open up your calendar instead. Then, add these two items to your schedule:

1. A ten-minute block of distraction-free time to do something *for you*. Alone. Yoga, a hot (quick) bath, a quick run, a quiet walk, time weeding the garden,

whatever. Don't fill this time with consuming content (no reading, TV, podcasts, etc.). Be conscious of where your mind goes as you enjoy this time.

2. A thirty-minute block to revisit this exercise. Sorry, there are no free passes on this one.

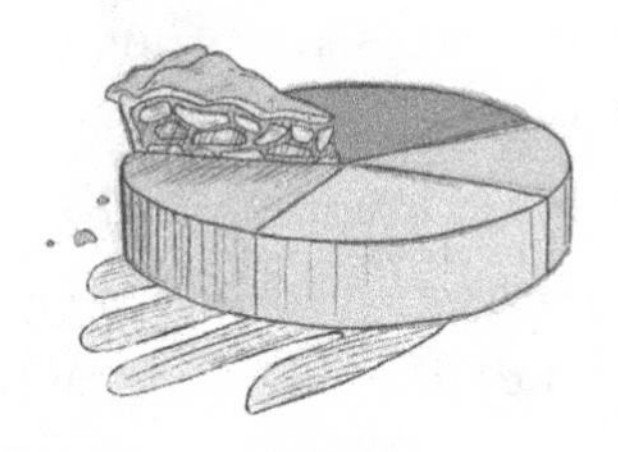

CHAPTER 3

EVEN SUPERMOM NEEDS HELP

Now that my daughter is twenty-one years old and "officially" grown, I can look back at things with a little more perspective. As I write this, Alaina is working for FEMA AmeriCorps, helping with personal protective equipment (PPE) logistics during the pandemic. She is far away, but I hear from her frequently by text.

Alaina also shares her Amazon wish list so I know what she's interested in for holiday gifts. Last week, I received three boxes from Amazon addressed to Alaina and I assumed that she had started Christmas shopping. Early in the week, I sent her a message to let her know that a box and two envelopes had arrived.

She texted back, "Can you open the box for me?"

To my surprise, it was a "just because" gift for me: a stemless wineglass printed with the saying, "Great Job Mom, I Turned Out Awesome." That is an amazing gift from your twenty-one-year-old who is halfway across the country doing hard work for little money. Her confidence, sense of humor, and appreciation all came through. It was a proud mom moment and everyone on Zoom that week saw it. In addition, when I opened the box, I realized that it was shipped from one of my clients who sells on Amazon. Sometimes life shows you, in the most creative ways, that you're doing what you're supposed to do.

I wasn't so confident in myself when Alaina was first born. New friends embraced us and were truly the family support I needed when I was so far from my North Carolina family and friends. This network was vital as I navigated days of nursing, changing diapers, and attending to a newborn's every need. The thirty-six weeks of a high-risk pregnancy, when days are filled with worries and your hands are mostly idle, don't prepare you for the constant attention that a newborn requires. I was overloaded from a lack of sleep and never getting a moment to myself. And while I couldn't imagine adding another thing to the list, something was missing.

After a time and with the help of my dear friend Katie, I realized that my brain was not getting the engagement it needed. Years of school and a professional life set me up to be an achievement junkie. Having multiple projects and balls in the air was fun for me, and I was good at it. Seeing an end result in my mind and recognizing the gap between it and a current state was like nourishment to my soul. I loved mapping out necessary steps and crossing things off the list as I made progress toward a goal. Now I asked myself different questions. *Can I get a nap in before she needs to nurse? Can I lay her down and have her stay asleep?* These were challenging times because I wanted nothing more than to be a great mom. I didn't want to work, but I was feeling so drained and incomplete. Parenting is a lifelong journey, and there is no way to know if you are doing a good job day by day or even week by week. While I tried not to dwell on that, I missed the sense of accomplishment in a job well done.

In addition to feeling tired and unfulfilled, I was also concerned about having those feelings. I felt guilty because I had exactly what I wanted and yet it wasn't enough. I had dreamed of idyllic days cuddling my child, pushing her in a stroller with girlfriends in the park, and having play dates. Yet my days were more like being too tired to feed myself. For someone used to juggling lots of balls, I was unable to keep my eye on the ball at all!

Another challenge centered around a feeling of emptiness and a lack of professional purpose. When you achieve something great, like giving life to a child or a book or accomplishing a big project, you feel empty afterwards. There is a sense of relief, but also a feeling of being a bit lost about what's next. With motherhood, all that attention and focus toward producing a result had now diffused into daily survival. I couldn't fathom doing anything else because I was barely getting by. And yet I was empty, and I needed something more—or at least something different.

Friends helped me gain perspective on the fact that I was losing my identity as I tried to be supermom all alone. I needed to deal with the reality that my family was so far away, that my friends from home who were having babies and careers were not close. The moms in the town I landed in were in their late teens and early twenties. Professional moms in their mid-thirties didn't exist here. Luckily, the friends my age and older in my new town were experienced moms and they had wisdom.

They helped me realize that, as an older mom, I needed to fulfill other parts of my soul, too. Gardening helped; volunteering helped. They got me through those early years.

I didn't start my business until my daughter was nine years old. When she was an infant, I jumped into volunteering and found ways to grow as a person. These friends taught me the value of a network. When I worked in a corporate job, I always dreaded networking because I am an introvert. The dinners and golf games were always uncomfortable for me. Now, years later in my own business, I see the value of a strong network for a new mom. If not for my support system, I may not have had my full-circle, wineglass gift moment. That moment helped me see that I had been rewarded for my decision to put my personal values—for my child-centric home *and* my professional identity—first.

LIFE SUPPORT

When I left my job and moved halfway across the country, I was surprised to discover that having a lot of free time after working in a professional role didn't really feel like freedom. I was just waiting to start this new life. Expecting to be expecting, I didn't want to get a job that I would soon leave. I didn't want to take on too many commitments because I knew that motherhood would change everything.

This interval is when my network of friendships and parenting support started to grow. Though I didn't know it at the time, these friendships would be long-lasting. They would also turn into business relationships. When you are in a new situation, finding others who have been on that road before and are willing to accept you where you are is extremely important. These people help you see beyond your day-to-day to the bigger picture and the dreams you have for yourself and your family. It is an investment of time and energy to stay close with friends and neighbors, but they will be your lifeline, so make the investment.

In those months before I got pregnant, I had very little to do to fill my days. At first, getting the house set up and ensuring that the contractor finished took time. But after a couple of weeks, I was at a loss. My dear neighbor Katie helped me find my way. Katie realized that I couldn't see my place in this new world and that I needed to get out and contribute, feel useful. She connected me with Nancy, the youth coordinator at the YMCA, who invited me to help with the summer kids' camp.

What a culture shock! Moving from the Research Triangle Park area in North Carolina, which had the largest concentration of PhDs in the United States at the time and twenty-seven universities within thirty miles, I found myself with children whose mothers were barely out of high school.

I loved spending time with these kids. It was summer. It was fun for them to go on field trips and make crafts. I could tell I was ready to be a mom. While this experience gave me that confidence, it also built up my network.

Nancy has three children, all boys. I got to know them at camp. The oldest became my daughter's first babysitter. When we moved from Missouri to Arkansas, he made the trip with us and helped unpack and care for Alaina while I got things organized. Later, as we continued to keep in touch with Nancy and her family, we learned of the Rotary Youth Exchange. Nancy was the coordinator for her district, and all three boys spent their gap years in a foreign country. Learning from them about Mexico, Turkey, and Thailand fueled a sense of adventure for Alaina. When she was sixteen, she spent a year in Brazil as a Rotary foreign exchange student. Upon her return, she spent two years as a camp counselor for students leaving to go on exchange. These types of experiences shaped her and us as a family and gave us a broader perception of ourselves in the world.

You never really know how the friends who come into your life may bring vital information or a connection that you will benefit from later. Just as networking is helpful for business, it is also helpful for parenting and feeding your individual identity. The cool thing is that these worlds have often overlapped in my life. When someone moves from friend to business connection, or a work connection becomes a personal friend, we share in each other's lives at multiple levels and are both enriched.

My friendship with Nancy later turned into a business relationship. She and two of her friends decided to switch directions with their careers after their children were grown and founded Golden Bridges, a business that serves families with seniors in housing transition, in Quincy, Illinois. If you have an aging parent who needs help downsizing from their family home to a condo—or maybe it's time for skilled nursing home care and getting heirlooms to kids—Nancy's company provides the extra care to help seniors and their families navigate these changes with thoughtful concern for the family and their belongings. What a noble mission.

Today, my business helps Golden Bridges navigate the world of accounting. It's been a joy to see how my personal relationship with Nancy and her children has developed over twenty years.

Business is personal for both me and Nancy. How could it not be? We have too many years of friendship under our belts to push that aside and have hardball negotiations over a contract. We always want what is best for each other.

Talking with Nancy recently, I asked her for her take on our friendship and business relationship.

Nancy shared, "It's been eighteen years since Cyndi left Missouri. In that time, our friendship, business relationship, and support for one another have been enhanced much more than I could ever imagine. Our lives have taken many new directions: business ownership (both), children growing up and living unbelievably rewarding lives, divorce (me), and the death of family members (both). We have only been a phone call away, and yet we also make the effort to connect by meeting halfway or visiting one another's homes. No time seems to matter each time we reconnect. Relationships can take work, but with Cyndi, it is effortless. Through our mutual support, we make our lives better!"

When we make new friends and those friendships develop over the years, we can't map out the development. There is no roadmap to plan your journey. But by taking steps together, day by day, we do find ourselves at destinations. At these stops, we realize that we have in fact traveled down the road together, and that the trip was so much richer because we shared the journey. Our support for one another along the way builds confidence that our friendship will be there in the moments when we need someone to lean on.

PROGRESS NUGGET: *You've just read 14,101 words, which is about half the words a seven-year old would use to tell you about their favorite TV show!*

A SECURE JOB IS NOT A REPLACEMENT FOR A SUPPORT NETWORK

EVEN WHEN YOU HAVE GOOD support, you may still worry that you're unable to manage it all. A colleague of mine, Wendy, is a CPA who is originally from South Africa. She had her own practice when her daughter was born. Wendy is so talented and professional. You can count on her to get the job done well and with no nonsense. As a single mom, she was stretched thin with her business and, while she had a support network, she didn't feel it was strong enough to get her through the days when nothing worked. Imagine her beautiful South African accent as she explains her first three years of being a mom and a business owner.

"As an accountant, March 15th is a very big day for me. It's the day the corporate tax filings are due. My daughter Francesca was born on March 13th. I was up in the hallways in the hospital, telling the nurses, 'You have got to release me. I need to get home. I have extensions to file and I'm carrying this newborn baby up and out of here.' The nurses are saying, 'You know, ma'am, we have procedures in the hospital. You need to wait your turn.' And I'm saying, 'But you don't understand...'"

The first two years of Francesca's life were hard for Wendy. She was burned out. She struggled to pay for health insurance and a nanny to help her so she could run her business. It was all just too much.

"It was really key to have people who understood what my life was like, who could support me. One day, I was lying in bed, sick. I called a girlfriend for help. She was also a self-employed business owner. I was so sick I could not stand up. My friend didn't have a key to my house, and it was before the days of doorbell apps on your phone, where you can open your front door remotely. She had to climb over the wall and get into my backyard, to the sliding door of my bedroom. I crawled over to the door to let her in. It was in that moment that I said, 'This is too hard. I cannot support clients, support a child, and take care of myself.' Thankfully, my friend was available that day, but what if she had not been?"

Wendy decided that she needed a "regular, stable life," one where she could get paid to stay in bed when she was sick and not run herself ragged. She went back to a salaried job and hired a full-time nanny. She took a job with a firm that promised her that her role as a mom would be respected, and she'd have some flexibility in her schedule and control over the clients she served.

"Two weeks in, I was miserable," Wendy said. "Having been self-employed for six years before that, going into a job was so much harder than I imagined it would be. And I stuck it out for a year because I'm not a quitter and I needed the health insurance. It was soul-destroying. I would rush home for dinner at six-thirty. I would pray the babysitter would show up on time. It was none of the things that I thought a secure job would do for our lives."

After a year at her job, Wendy quit and went back into business for herself.

"When my self-employed clients tell me that they are tired, they 'can't do this anymore' and want to go get a job, I tell them my story. I want them to realize that the paycheck every two weeks is appealing, but the price is so incredibly high. For me, the price was missing my daughter's day. I'd leave the house very early in the morning and come home very late at night, so tired. And I dealt with clients I didn't choose in corporate environments and structures that did not bring me joy. It took such a toll."

With Wendy's second child, she did things differently. She had gone back to her own accounting firm when her son was born. This time, though, she had a very supportive spouse. She was home for eight days and then handed the baby back to her husband and said, "I love this child, but I have got to get back to work. I can no longer wear a robe." Her husband stayed home with her son for three months and did all the heavy lifting. Support can come in many forms. Be sure to look for what is available to support you.

Wendy shared, "If I could give one piece of advice to entrepreneurial moms, it would be: Don't give up, don't give up! I gave up and went back to a job, and it cost me a year of misery. You can do this."

I too know you can do this, and it will be much smoother when you find those people who can support you. They are out there. In fact, Julie, a periodontist and mom from Kansas City, shared that there is a network of people who are actually good at this because they do it so frequently.

"Military parents are better at this than the rest of us because they're used to moving frequently," Julie said. "When you move, the first thing you do is get to your new place and meet your neighbors. You figure out who you can count on."

AJ, whom you met in the last chapter, was determined not to go back to a full-time office job after she had her son. She started a freelance writing business, which quickly shifted into ghostwriting books. To grow her business, she relied heavily on her mom support network—both when her son was still a toddler and in the years that followed. She found a local organization that provided a space for moms to bring their toddlers and talk with other moms while the kids played. There, she met several parents who would become the center of her network.

"On any given day, if I needed a couple of hours to work, or if I was running late from a meeting, I could call at least fifteen moms who could meet my son's bus or take him to baseball practice," AJ told me. "And I would do the same for them. Maybe I'd take their kids home *from* baseball practice. Or we'd swap some other duties. That's how we all stayed present for our kids and managed to keep up with our work."

If it works for our other families, it will work for you, too. You simply need to tap into a network that will give you the support you need. Don't give up until you find one. And if you can't find one, start one!

SUPPORT HELPS YOU STAY HEALTHY

From the vantage point of daily childcare, it's not easy to see past the next load of laundry, the next diaper, or the next meal. I encourage you to set aside some time for yourself anyway. Use that time to take care of your physical and mental health. As moms, we're all about our families and we tend to miss the all-important message that the family will be fine if Mom is fine. The airlines have had this figured out for years. You know, that part in the safety demonstration when the flight attendant tells you, "In the event of an emergency, put your oxygen mask on first and then help your child." I know, you didn't pay attention to that either; we're too busy getting our child's iPad set up during the announcement. Well, it's good advice, so pay attention to it now.

You want what is best for your child, so don't compromise your own well-being to achieve that. I say this from the position of being an "over-giver." As a new parent, I didn't set boundaries very well or take care of my health. Luckily, my genes are sturdy and strong and helped me get through the inadequate self-care, but we never know what impact we're having on our later years. To the extent I put boundaries in place, my network helped me find a way to find that time for myself. If you don't have a strong network, perhaps you are a more introspective person and need space to think so you can get clear on your needs and boundaries.

When the day-to-day seems like too much, finding the time to think or do something that fulfills you is critical. Your network can help you find time to devote to your thoughts, and you can also structure your day so that you have that kind of time.

YOUR PROFESSIONAL NETWORK CAN HELP YOU CREATE THE LIFE YOU WANT

SOMETIMES, EVEN WITH THE HELP of a parent support group, you still end up with the short end of the stick, last on your list. AJ's ghostwriting business—and support from her spouse and her mom network—allowed her to create a child-centric home for her son, the kind she didn't have growing up. She had the flexibility to be there for her son, Jack. However, ghostwriting eight to ten books a year was very demanding and draining. She constantly had books in various stages of completion and would work when Jack was sleeping or at school. Her life became ghostwriting and caring for Jack. As a result, she lost sight of caring for herself and her relationship with her spouse.

This imbalance of her time reached a point where it could not be ignored. She and her wife were on their annual summer vacation, which coincided with their wedding anniversary. "I was supposed to take a drive around with my wife, which is something we love to do," AJ told me. "She went to town and I took the opportunity to sneak in some work. When she got back to the cabin, I was on the phone with work. She knew that, if I was on the phone, it could be an hour. She said, 'That's it!' We got in a huge argument, and I remember saying to myself, *Okay, you might be doing fine on being there for your kid, but you're not there for your wife.*

"I was that mom at every game, every doctor appointment, every everything. I was overkill on it. Even if she could be there, I would still be there. I didn't want him to feel abandoned by me—even though he had two moms and she could carry some of the load. Finally, the you-know-what hit the fan and I had to say to myself, *Okay, you are not functioning in the right way here.* And I knew I had to give up ghostwriting because it wasn't working in my life, I wasn't healthy. I put on probably like a hundred pounds. And I decided I had to quit."

AJ is the writing partner to Mike Michalowicz, author of *Profit First* and other business books. She told him she planned to quit ghostwriting but wanted to keep writing with him. Beyond that, she had no plan. She was floundering and unsure where to turn.

Then Mike asked her to help him coach students at a book retreat he had created with Michael Port, founder of Heroic Public Speaking and author of *Steal the Show* and other books.

"The experience of being at that retreat gave me a new way of looking at my work. As I helped people with their book ideas, I began to understand the reasons I was successful as a ghostwriter—not just because I could become the voice of my clients, but also because I could draw things out of them and help them organize their thoughts around a clear message. Up until that retreat, I didn't know that I could do that."

The book retreat gave AJ the opportunity to see her path forward and her skills in a different light. She also had a great mentor to hold up the mirror.

As AJ and Mike made the return trip home, she had a new vision for herself. "I remember thinking in the car, *Wow, this is fun. I can do this, and I could have a life!* I started to see my way forward."

This event set a number of things in motion. Soon after the retreat, AJ joined the faculty at Heroic Public Speaking and started taking private clients to coach through book writing. Now she teaches courses and retreats of her own. This new business model developed because she faced the fact that she had to do something different for herself and her family. And if you like any part of this book, it's because AJ is brilliant and gave me great direction in my courses with her.

"I had so wanted to be there for my son in a way that my parents weren't there for me, but I had to change the parameters so that I could also be there for my wife, and myself. Because if you're working seven days a week, you skip you. You stop working and go to a game, stop working for family dinner, stop working to take your kid to a birthday party, stop working to do all that stuff and pick them up from school. That doesn't mean you're not working too much. It just means you've put him first. Then you work for the rest of the time. And there's nothing left after that."

Fulfilling her goal of creating a child-centric home took a toll on AJ's health and her relationships. She was forced into her Sacred Space by her spouse, who was at the end of her rope. She took the time to examine her life and stepped out with faith that she would find a better way.

AJ has a strong professional network, with successful authors like Mike Michalowicz and Michael Port who helped her see her skills in a new way. Your network wants to help you. We all want to share our experiences to help someone that may be behind us on the path. It doesn't matter if that path is mothering or building a business. Letting others know what you're struggling with allows them to share their gifts. And if you're considering it a weakness to ask for help, it's actually a sign of maturity.

These tactics of developing and using your network and taking time for reflection give you the space to think about what you need and what your family needs. Sometimes that will lead to changes in how you structure your routine or how you use your network for support. It may even allow you the chance to see how to reinvent your business model. The key is that these moments of misalignment or imbalance happen in your personal life and in your business life, and if you have made Sacred Space, you will see them as possibilities. It's critical for entrepreneurs to get out of the busy-ness so that they can consider long-term direction and strategy, and maybe even reinvent their businesses. These skills carry over into both realms, which makes us better in both.

PROGRESS NUGGET: *You've just finished fifty-five pages, rock star. When will you read the next five?*

GET READY TO HAVE IT ALL

As I said in Chapter 1, yes, you can have it all—and it's better for you and everyone in your life if you do. Of course, that's easier said than done, which is why so many moms never manage to get there. The good news—the really *great* news—is, you now have two crucial strategies that will help you figure out what you want your life to look like and help you get as close to that vision as possible: Sacred Space and a support network. With these tools, you will find that this important work of building the life you want is so much easier. Take the time to incorporate both into your daily life and you will reap rewards that you were only able to imagine before.

DEFINE YOUR SUPPORT NETWORK

- **Suggested Time to Complete:** Twenty minutes, plus time to meaningfully connect with your network.

- **When you complete this exercise,** you will have identified your support system, and they will know how grateful you are for them. Then, when "life happens," you'll know who to call.

⊗ **If you skip this exercise**, you will be in a bind when you inevitably encounter conflicts or knowledge gaps. This exercise is like creating an insurance policy for your personal and business lives.

In her book, *Becoming,* Michelle Obama wrote that "Friendships between women... are built of a thousand small kindnesses... swapped back and forth and over again."[11] It's time to create a list of the people in your life whom you can rely on for help, advice, or some other small kindness as a mom, human, and business owner.

If you find the notion of asking for help difficult, remember that relationships—whether personal or business—are two-way connections. If knowing *you* didn't benefit and brighten the lives or businesses of the people on the lists you're about to make, you probably wouldn't even be thinking of them right now.

First, focus on your personal network of supporters. These are trusted family members, friends, and colleagues who are available to you. Aim to write down at least three people for your personal network and three for your business network—more is great.

1. Create a list of situations in which you might need to call on someone to help you. For example:
    a. Your meeting with a client is running late. Who can you text to meet your child at the bus stop?

   b. You're helping an elderly relative recover from surgery. Who can watch your child so that you can help your relative?
   c. You know that you're more productive and a happier human when you can make it to yoga class twice a week. Who can help make this happen?
2. In the situations you listed, who can you call on for help? Think of your friends, family, and other parents in your circle. Try not to rely too heavily on one or two people. Take special care to not rely too heavily on your spouse or partner if you have one.
3. Your list can also include resources available to you. For example, my local YMCA offered members two hours of childcare per day. That's two hours of child-free work time! You might research options like drop-in childcare or sick-child care to see if these options are available in your area. Contact these places and form a relationship with them before you need them.
4. Next, call or have coffee with your supporters to talk about your plans and ambitions and ask for their support in the ways you've listed. As you do this, be sure to express your gratitude to them for the role they play in your life. Then, if appropriate to the situation, offer to reciprocate regularly or ad hoc (e.g., with occasional childcare).

Again, remember that most people *want* to be helpful and see you succeed. Other parents, especially, will understand your situation and want to support you. In life and in business, it really *is* true that we get by with a little help from our friends.

MY PERSONAL NETWORK		
What situation might I need help with?	**Who can help?**	**Did I ask them and show gratitude?**
If I have a meeting that runs late, I might not make it to school pickup on time.	Tessa or Emily, if they are also at the bus stop. My mom.	Yes!

Next, repeat the steps above for your business network. Think of situations in which you may need help or advice to get over a hurdle or to the next level. Again, be sure to consider resources that may be available to you in addition to people.

MY BUSINESS NETWORK		
What situation might I need help with?	**Who can help?**	**Did I ask them and show gratitude?**
I'm having trouble picking a final logo from the selection the designer sent me. I really want to get this right, since my business has grown enough that I'm ready to purchase signage.	Cora fits the profile of my target customer and works in marketing. I can ask her. Thomasina is a graphic designer. I can pick her brain over coffee.	Yes!
I keep running into an error in QuickBooks.	Delia is a bookkeeper.	Yes! We are meeting on Wednesday. I'll write a thank you note and bring some chocolates to go with it.

⧗ **Fast Five:** If you don't have the time or space to complete this exercise right now, do this instead:

Personal Network: Think of *two* people (other than your partner) whom you can rely on in a personal emergency. Make sure you have their contact info in your phone.

Business Network: Think of *one* person you can go to with business questions. Open your calendar and schedule ten minutes to reach out to them sometime in the next seven days.

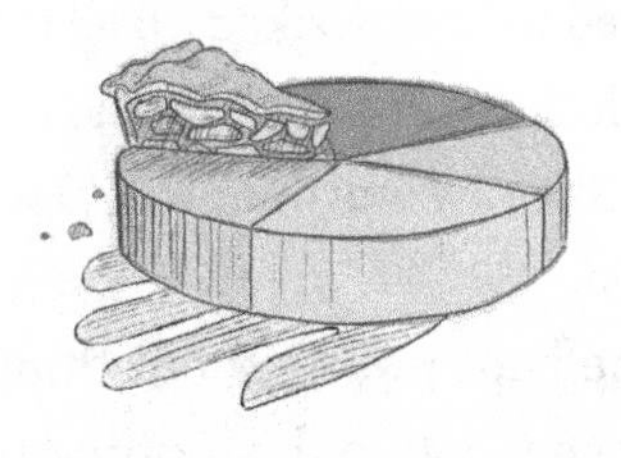

CHAPTER 4
MODEL YOUR PURPOSE FOR YOUR CHILD

WHEN I FIRST STARTED INTRODUCING my clients to Profit First, a cash management methodology developed by Mike Michalowicz,[12] I had the opportunity to speak to a group of creative professionals at a conference in Fayetteville, Arkansas. Alaina and I decided to make a fun day of it. I'd speak at my event and then we'd explore and have fun.

Fifteen at the time, Alaina didn't really understand or seem to pay much attention to what I did for work. This was an opportunity to show her.

During my speech, she sat quietly on the floor in the back of the auditorium and watched.

When I was done, we walked to join friends for lunch, and Alaina gushed compliments.

She said, "Mom, that was fun, and they loved you."

She told me about how excited she was to see the audience respond to my ideas. She talked about how engaged they seemed. She seemed to have soaked up all the positive energy in the room. I could tell from the way she talked that she saw me in a new light. She saw worth in what I was doing and the impact I could have.

Over lunch, she kept pointing out things I'd said in the speech. "Mom, when you told the toothpaste story, everyone got it. You should give out toothpaste." And, "Mom, when you talked about the new profit formula, everyone wrote that down."

Alaina had heard what I had to share and was processing it from a different perspective. It was the first time we had an interaction about work that showed she saw me as someone vibrant and active. Most days, she saw me sitting at a desk, staring at a screen and talking on a conference call. Not too impressive to an active young person. When she could see the impact of my work and sense the energy in the room, she could relate to me and my professional life with more understanding.

Because of this interaction, I became aware that she was watching, and that I had been modeling what work was like for adults. I could be in a behind-the-scenes role or I could be out front; that didn't matter. Living my life to its fullest mattered—because she was watching.

There are no right or wrong answers about your pursuits or passions, and I make no judgments here about anyone's choices. I simply want to raise your awareness of the small audience you have during this special time in your lives. Our children are watching—even when we think they aren't. I want you to make the most of their attention, and through the stories in this chapter, you'll learn a few ways to do that.

SET THE STAGE FOR SELF-DISCOVERY

SEVEN YEARS AGO, MY DEAR friend Marge was ordained to the priesthood. A special Episcopal service celebrated her accomplishment in study, blessed her for this important work, and sent her off into her new role. The sermon was delivered by one of Marge's sponsors in the church, Father Harv Sanders. The words he spoke resonated with me, and I have thought of them often on my business journey. They made me think differently about myself and about the role of work in my life. He said, "No vocation is simply about activity. Vocation is as much about identity as it is about activity."

To illustrate this point, Father Sanders used the wonderful children's book, *What Do People Do All Day?* by Richard Scarry.[13] "Scarry was a master at depicting what a plumber does, but how could he possibly have drawn a picture of who a plumber is? If you ask most people what they do for their life's work, they will usually respond with an answer that has to do with identity. They will usually respond with an 'I am' statement. I am a teacher. I am a doctor. I am a carpenter. I am a farmer. The longer a person is involved in a vocation, the deeper that sense of self-identity becomes. All of us here this evening have been formed by our various vocations. If you had made a different choice years ago about your life's work, you would be a very different person from what you are today. Vocational identity does not come in an instant. It happens over a period of time. [Marge's] vocation has been developing over the years, but from this point on it will be very different. From the point of ordination on, we start to look at ourselves differently, and others start to look at us differently."

As you consider your vocation, remember, it's not just an activity. It's an aspect of your identity. What job or business will give you the most joy, happiness, and fulfillment? While opening a business is not for everyone, and some moms are happy to dedicate themselves to mothering full-time or divide their time between family and a job, there is a group of us that seeks something different—something that allows us to put our mark on the world and say, "This is what I want to create and how I want to work and serve others."

Have you considered the impact you want to have on the world? There is so much to consider with starting or growing a business that you can get bogged down in the day-to-day responsibilities and forget to take stock. The same is true of being a mom—you will be busy. Be deliberate about your life and set aside time to think about how you want to show up in this world. This time is part of your Sacred Space; don't neglect it. If you do, you risk losing your anchor on this journey.

I participate in a couple of business organizations that help me continue to grow both personally and professionally. One of the best exercises I did recently was led by Donald Miller, author of *Building a StoryBrand*. It required us to consider how long we expect to live and to get our heads around how many years we actually have left. Donald, like me, is a dog lover, and he put this question in terms that resonated: "Dogs live about twelve years. How many dogs do you have left?" When I thought about each of our dogs over the years and the things that were happening in our lives while they were with us, this way of marking time made sense. The key here is to pick an interval that helps you grasp the passage of time and consider what you want to accomplish.

How do you want to be remembered? Is there a purpose you want to put your energy into to make a difference in your community? The culmination of Miller's thought exercise was for us to write our own obituaries. This is a bit sobering to think through, but I guarantee that it will give you clarity.

Writing my obituary prompted me to write this book. I became crystal clear about my vision for my business, which is to give more opportunities to team members so they can create better integration between work and other pursuits, such as family or school. I became clear about the importance of education in my life. I realized that my involvement in the business needed to be more closely aligned with my personal vision. I knew that education, as a big part of my why, was important for my role in the business with both my team and my clients.

I know that when you work through the questions at the end of this chapter, you too will have clarity around how you want to show up as a mom.

YOUR SMALL AUDIENCE

KIDS WILL ALWAYS BE MORE interested in themselves, but they do like to see their moms doing something they love. When our day-to-day work doesn't show the impact of what we do, we need to find ways to convey that to them. It's just human nature to complain about work and what is challenging or not going right. Think about your small audience every day. Be sure to let them know about your wins, what makes you happy, and how what you do has an impact on other people. A fun way to do this is to include them in your celebrations as you meet important milestones at work. My colleague and friend Susanne, an author and CPA based in Houston, explained to me, "They're only little once—make sure you have fun with them. Every week that my book was number one on the new release list, we had a celebration that Friday. When my company turned ten years old, I took them on a Disney cruise. I was showing them that when you work hard, you get to have bigger rewards, and I like to correlate the work with the fun."

Let your child in on your "why"—the reason you chose your vocation. This will set the expectation for them that, when they choose a vocation, they will have a why, too.

My why has a strong learning and educating component. It's a part of me that comes out whether I'm working or volunteering. I just believe in the "Teach a man to fish" parable. It goes back to my childhood and my grandfather, whom we called Pop. He left school when he was in the third grade because his father died. Pop had to help support his mom and his brothers and sisters. He worked his way up the ladder at his job to become a supervisor at a coal-fired electricity plant, but he could barely read.

After school, I would come home and then go across the road to see my grandparents. This was the scene: Pop would be sitting at the counter in the kitchen, sounding out words in the newspaper. My grandmother, cooking dinner, would turn from her work to help him as he practiced reading. I would sit beside him and help him, too.

Throughout my entire life and on each visit, he made the same point: "Get your education. No one can ever take that away from you."

When I was in grade school, he asked about my report card and gave me a quarter for every "A." When I was working full-time and going to college part-time, he'd always ask about my schoolwork. Because college was part-time, it took me eleven years to complete my bachelor's degree. During my visits over those eleven years, he'd always ask, "What are you learning?" and "How are your grades?" Even as an adult in college, I got a quarter for each "A."

Out of Pop's eight grandchildren, I was the only one who graduated college. I was driven and motivated because he impressed the importance of education on me. He modeled learning and rewarded me often, even though it was with just a token; and this ritual is one of my special memories of Pop.

I explained this story to Alaina, and how the lock screen picture on my phone of her induction into an honors program at college reminds me not only of her accomplishment, but my part in it and Pop's part in the value I place on education. It's why I love working with clients and team members to help them connect the dots on how to improve their businesses or some aspect of their work. Guiding my team and my clients to lightbulb moments is my why. Sharing it with Alaina helps to set the stage for her own self-discovery.

HOW DOES YOUR CHILD SEE YOU?

While it's important to consider what we want to accomplish in the business or professional world, I think the role of motherhood deserves its own exercise. At most, you probably only have about twenty high-involvement years in this role. And when your child starts going to school, then driving, then working a part-time job, your time to make your mark grows shorter. How do you want your child to remember their childhood, to remember you as their mom?

The exercise is at the end of the chapter, but to set the stage for it, imagine that your child is about seventeen years old and you overhear them talking to a new friend. In this "getting to know you" conversation, your child is describing you. He is proud of you. You are surprised by all the details he notices. In the exercise, take a moment to write down what you want to hear your child say to this new friend. This description will be your goalpost or your Ideal State. You will see the end goal, and you will also see the gap you have to close. If you don't have children yet, this exercise will help you imagine your new role as a mom and what that might look like through your child's eyes.

Once you know the gap, you can start to make plans to close it and create a True Vision for your life and work. Decide on the big goals and projects you have for your mom role. Maybe you want to demonstrate how you are present with your child when you are together, so you create a "no phone" rule. Or maybe homecooked meals and family dinners are important to how you show up for your family. Maybe you want your kids to learn self-care. How will they perceive your own self-care? Do they see you prioritize exercise and making healthy food choices for yourself? What do they witness with your friendships? Do you show a giving side, or are you always looking to find fault or for what you can get from your friends? You will want them to describe your work, too. Do they see you as being committed and fueled by purpose? This is a sample of the questions you will answer in the exercise at the end of this chapter. Your responses will set the stage for how you parent, how you work, and how you make the two aspects of your life work together.

Make the time to give this exercise the consideration it deserves. The next fifteen to twenty years will fly by, and you will need to revisit this vision document as you, your child, and your family situations change. Refer to the results of your exercises when you're feeling anxious and stressed or as you make decisions. Evaluate what is causing the anxiety by reviewing your current situation and desired outcome. The gap will be apparent, and you will have more clarity about the next steps you can take to close it.

You may be overwhelmed by the results of this exercise. There may be many changes you want to make. Don't attempt too much at first; we can't do a makeover of our behaviors like they do with makeup and hair on TV. Think about how to stage the changes you want to make and pick two to three things to focus on at a time. Too many changes or projects mean you will focus on nothing. Only one means that you're often on pause, waiting for something. If you constantly have two or three goals or projects to work on, you will always be making progress.

MAKE YOUR OWN WAY

One of the reasons these exercises are so important is that they put you in touch with what you want. It's so easy to get caught up in what society says we should do, what we see on TV commercials, what our friends are doing, and what our family expects from us. While all these perspectives are data inputs, you get to write your program. You get to decide what will work best for you and your family. This time in your life—and your child's—is too important for you to follow someone else's path.

Femke is the owner and official licensee of Profit First Professionals Netherlands, where she resides and operates a thriving financial consultancy. There are more than sixty-eight Profit First Professionals under her wing, which is phenomenal in such a small country. She explains that, as an older mother, she was not part of a circle of friends who experienced pregnancy and maternity together. She also has a very can-do attitude and didn't look to others for advice. Because she didn't have other moms to compare herself to, she never questioned whether she would breastfeed her child or not. It made sense to her that she would, so she did.

"Later, I found out that there's a whole world around the whole breastfeeding issue; if you should or should not," Femke said. "There's a whole world about how difficult it is and how much a hassle and what if he doesn't want to drink. I didn't have all that. I just breastfed, that's it."

Sometimes when we look to others for answers, we become paralyzed. While many moms help and support, others tear down. As you continue to develop your support network, make sure your community is supportive and weed out those who aren't.

Laura, the Australian mom who worked through business decisions while walking with her child in the stroller, puts more value on her kids' opinions of her decisions than the negative opinions of other moms. Her older son is proud of her work and because her businesses are all related to finances. "He understands that you need money to live, and now he is earning pocket money through chores," she said. "He's making decisions with that money and talking openly about it when most kids his age are just like, 'What?' Sometimes other parents judge me because they see him as being money-driven. But it's not that. He's been exposed to my industry and how I encourage people to make decisions." Laura's son is not only learning good work habits from the example his mom is setting, he is learning about the nature of her business.

You decide what is best for you and your family—when it comes to both mothering and your business. Your life is a blank canvas. Artists are influenced by other artists and the masterworks, but in the end, they create art from a place within their heart and soul. You have the same opportunity.

Completing these exercises is the first step in making your own way. To stay true to your journey, you will need to come back to your True Vision on a regular basis. I review mine every week as I prepare for the week ahead. This habit allows me to consider: *Is this still the right path? Am I still doing the most important things to move me forward? Did I learn something from my friends that will cause me to make an adjustment?*

If not, you continue to move forward as planned. And because you have carefully considered your path, you can articulate your position to those who offer their well-meaning but nonapplicable advice in a non-defensive way. If the advice is valuable, then you can adjust. The important thing to remember is that you get to choose. You are the one setting an example for your child, so be sure you're in harmony with your path.

SET AN EXAMPLE

When Alaina was a baby and we lived in Missouri, I participated in a parenting program called Parents as Teachers.

The Missouri Department of Education realized that education started well before kindergarten. They knew that, as parents, we are our children's first teachers.

Those big character lessons in life, you'll be teaching those to your child before they ever go to school. Initially, the lessons come from watching you. Kids are like little computers, observing every action, processing what makes us smile and what upsets us. As they get older and start to establish separation and independence, they know how to pull all the levers and push all the buttons. They are watching everything. When we are overwhelmed and unfulfilled, they sense and feel our emotions.

I recall being so anxious when my mother- and father-in-law were coming to visit. My daughter was a tiny baby, maybe a month or two old, and I was still nursing. I tried hard to have it all together, but she was fussy the entire time. Even though I looked cool on the outside, she knew I was not cool on the inside. Children pick up on everything, even when we are calm on the surface and struggling on the inside.

Sharon is a CPA in Alberta, Canada. When I interviewed her for this book, she explained that she left a larger accounting practice a few years ago when her children were very young. We talked about her kids—Scarlet, ten, and Oliver, seven—and their perception of her as a working mom. She shared that they appreciate the freedom and "power" of her being a business owner. They say, "You're the boss, Mommy! You can take the day off and you can tell people what to do."

Of course, to kids so young, the appearance of power doesn't necessarily convey the accompanying responsibility. Sharon said, "Growing a business is teaching your kids valuable life lessons, like showing that you're a strong woman who goes out there, takes action, and builds something for herself, rather than just doing what other people think she should do."

Sharon grew up on a farm in Canada. Her mom was home during the day and always there after school. When Sharon was in junior high school, her mom decided to go back to university to become a teacher. She had to drive three hours to get to her classes and was gone three days a week.

"Mom felt guilty for not being there," Sharon told me. "She always thought that she was kind of abandoning us a little bit, but in our eyes, we saw her as going after her dreams. It's kind of funny how she had that perception that we felt abandoned or neglected because, as her children, we noticed she was gone, but we weren't abandoned. Dad took over and that was fine."

As moms, we take on the guilt and think we know how our actions are going to impact every family member. But Sharon remembers that, as children, she and her brother thought it was so cool that Mom was "going for it!"

Sharon said, "My mom set a great example of putting herself first, and that inspired me to see myself as both a professional and a mom."

If only we could see through the lens of our future selves that we can ditch the guilt and get on with setting a great example.

Sharon's story also shows how her parents worked together to take care of the family and give her mother the space to pursue her teaching degree and later become a teacher. This support from her spouse made it work from all sides. It also set up the same expectation, and now experience, that Sharon has in her marriage.

Sharon really hustled to create her CPA practice. After a year of maternity leave, which is standard in Canada, she came back to work expecting to be on partner track. But things had changed for her boss, and he no longer wanted to add a partner in the business. Sharon was convinced that she wanted to set her own rules and be her own boss. With the partner door closed, she decided to start her own business during downtime at work and in the evenings after the kids went to bed. It took her a couple of years, and when her side revenue was enough to cover her expenses, she left the CPA business.

She remembers how the first few tax seasons were really challenging for her. She had to enroll her children in afterschool sports and activities to help manage all the extra work hours she faced. She talked with her husband about the stress and her concerns, and they worked out a plan for him to step in after school, giving her room to work and ensuring that the kids were not overscheduled.

Sharon said that understanding your boundaries and communication are key to working out this arrangement. "Be open with your partner about your struggles and share the workload when it comes to the household. One reason I am successful is because my husband helps around the house. He cleans, gets groceries, runs the kids around. There are no blue/pink jobs in our house; we both pick up the slack when needed. If I didn't have that support at home and had to do all the household stuff too, I would be wiped out and have no energy for my business."

In addition to making their household work, Sharon and her husband are setting an example for their children. They are showing their kids that parents should support each other, and that gender roles around chores are not useful for their family or how they work together to ensure that everyone gets the care and support they need. Sharon models that it's okay to ask for help when you need it. The kids notice the results she gets from working with her husband, and there is no doubt that this will help them when they have relationships of their own.

> PROGRESS NUGGET: *Did you know that the average horse produces about fifty pounds of horseshit a day? Remember this when your child asks for a pony.*

MODELING YOUR VALUES

JULIA IS A LAWYER BY training. She has worked in communications and is now an ecommerce business owner. When she shared her story for this book, it was evident that she and her husband had considered their every behavior as modeling, from the daily moments with their children to the implications of their business offerings out in the world.

When Julia's husband Jeremy contacted me for help with Profit First years ago, he was developing a plan to spend more time at home with their children, Josephine (JoJo) and Wilder. At the time, JoJo was three and Wilder was a newborn. It was important to Jeremy to walk his kids to and from school. We developed a plan that allowed his family to live off the income from their ecommerce store.

When I interviewed Julia, she and Jeremy were both working from home due to the global pandemic, and the kids were remote learning. This disruption inspired Julia to give a lot of thought to the interrelationship of business and parenting.

"Being a mom makes me a better business owner because I ask myself, *How can I have more of an impact on the world?* When we published our baby journal, there was a question of whether we would get pushback because it is an LGBTQ-friendly baby journal and putting it out there in the world and marketing it that way. I said to myself, *This is the world I want my kids to grow up in. I want them to grow up in an inclusive world. I believe in an inclusive world; we're going to push for that. If it flops, it flops. If we get pushback, we get pushback; but it's the right thing to be pushing against.* We went forward with that intent."

Why not use our business platforms to help solve some of the societal issues we consider important? Laura, Sharon, and I have seen the need for flexibility in the workplace for women and we have made it part of our businesses' cultures to provide that for our team members.

Julia also considered how she and Jeremy show up and are influenced by society. While the traditional corporate path was available to both of them, they decided to really examine what they wanted for their family and how they could achieve it.

Julia said, "We're also modeling how to live on our terms, that we don't have to follow along with what society says is valuable. Our expendable income would be higher if Jeremy and I had stayed in the corporate world, but we'd have a whole lot less freedom. We want to help the kids see that and use it as a model as they make their own decisions in life.

"Society tells me that money, and a big house and more money, and then more money is always the right choice. Society says that if I'm not working twelve hours a day, I'm not working hard enough. That sort of thing. When I was going into a legal career, there was the expectation that if you were going to be a good lawyer and get paid a lot, you were going to work yourself just to the bone. But it's okay to step back and say, 'That's not what I want my life to be, that's not where I'm going to put my value, and that's not what I think. That's not my decision,' and then choose an alternate path."

There is so much opportunity now to do things our own way if we take the time to consider what we really value. From a business perspective, barriers to starting a business are minimal in so many sectors now. Technology has opened up opportunities in online sales, remote teams, and the gig economy, just to name a few areas. This is your opportunity to consider how you want your business to show up in the world and how you want to show up for your kids.

Julia told me that her work as a business owner also provides lots of learning opportunities for her kids. For example, she is teaching them the concept of independence and how to embrace the "start where you are, use what you have, and do what you can" attitude.

She said, "It's a brave thing to start a business. It's important to remember that because when you do, you end up in entrepreneurship circles and with all these other folks in your masterminds; you surround yourself with those people and you forget that initial courage you had. It's important to remember that starting a business is not necessarily a common thing to do." According to data gathered by LegalZoom in 2020, roughly 15 percent of adults in the US are business owners.[14]

Julia continued, "It requires taking chances. I hope my kids are getting the message that it's good to take chances on things that are important to you, and to try, and also to fail. That failure is okay. It doesn't make you a bad person. It doesn't make you a failure. You tried something and it didn't go over well. Okay. It doesn't define you. You just get up, dust yourself off, and move on from it. You keep trying. That resiliency piece is important, and we are modeling that. Hopefully they're picking up on it."

Julia shared with me that while she and Jeremy see the importance of these lessons for their kids, it doesn't mean that their chosen path is easy. Like all parents, they deal with the stress of doing it all. Homeschooling their children during the pandemic gave the kids more of an opportunity to see what their parents' work life is like, and it required Jeremy and Julia to be flexible and bring their support for each other to a new level. I love that they go on a long weekend trip every month as a family just to get a change of pace from being at home all the time. What a great strategy they developed to help them all cope with this unusual challenge. Working together to determine what you need can lead you to some interesting places!

Each of the women in this book determined a path for mothering and set off in that direction determined to make her business work to fit her needs. Each of them realized that she needed her business to help her become who she wanted to be in the world in addition to a mom. Their paths are more like curvy roads than straight lines because often, what we think we want has changed when we arrive at our goals. Our True Vision for how we work and mother becomes the starting point from which to make adjustments. If you have to change a part of that vision, it doesn't mean that you didn't think about it enough or make a good enough plan. It simply means that the destination looked different once you arrived. If you researched a hotel before making a trip and it looked great and had good reviews but didn't live up to your expectations when you arrived, you'd adjust. Maybe you'd change hotels or shorten your stay. You wouldn't beat yourself up; it just didn't work, so you'd make a change. Give yourself that grace as you navigate these big decisions.

Our expectations are rooted in our experience growing up, our partner's experience growing up, societal norms, our families' influence, and our hopes and dreams. It's a lot to digest—and then you add hormones and finances to the mix! Don't lose yourself in this process. Keep checking in and moving forward. Following your passion will benefit you and your children. Your purpose will be fulfilled, and the example you set for your children will be noticed. It will be part of what shapes them into tomorrow's adults.

YOU IN YOUR CHILD'S EYES

Suggested Time to Complete: Thirty minutes.

When you complete this exercise, you will have a True Vision of how you want your future relationship with your child(ren) to look. That vision will inform the actions you should take today to make it happen.

If you skip this exercise, you miss an opportunity to set—or at least evaluate—the foundations for your future relationship with your child(ren) and priorities for your family time.

How do you want to be seen in the eyes of your child or children? Caution: This is not where you simply say, "I want to be best friends with my child once they are an adult." This is deep work. It's time to get intentional about the important lessons you want your child to learn *and how you want them to see you as a parent and role model.* Your answers to these questions should represent your Ideal State, or the relationship you would *like* to have with your child. Let's jump in!

Step 1: Create time and space for this exercise.

What you put into this exercise will determine what you get out of it. Reserve twenty to thirty minutes to answer the following questions. Permit yourself to spend more time on the exercise if you find it speaks to you.

Step 2: Envision your almost-adult child.

Think about what your child will be like when they are a senior in high school, on the cusp of adulthood, and, perhaps, leaving the nest for their next stage in what will be a bright life. Ask yourself:

- Do they enjoy school and learning? How would their teachers, coaches, or tutors describe them?
- What will the next few years of their life bring? Will they go to college or trade school, enter the workforce, or take a gap year?
- What do they like to do with their friends? Do they enjoy spending time with their family?
- What are the traditions and rituals that form the cornerstones of your life as a family?

Step 3: What would they say about you?

Are you feeling incredibly proud of the almost-adult child you envisioned in Step 2? With that image in mind, it's time to turn your attention back to you. In this step, you will look at yourself through your child's eyes. What would they say about you, your career, and your family? Remember, your answers should describe your Ideal State, or the relationship you would *ideally* have with your child.

- How would your child describe the work that you do? Do they see you enjoying your work and feeling good about your impact on the world?
- How much time do you spend together? Chances are, your teen will have a packed schedule between school, extracurricular activities, and their social life. What is the time you spend together like? How are you present and holding space for your child?
- What are your conversations with your child like? Do they speak openly with you and seek your guidance? Or do conflicts overshadow your relationship?

Step 4: Roadmap your relationship.

The Ideal State from Steps 2 and 3 is your destination. To arrive there, you will need to set the correct trajectory for your parenting *now.* First, look at your answers from the previous steps and honestly assess your current state.

For example, if you'd like your child to say, someday: "My family always made time to connect, even when things were busy. Sunday mornings were sacred: We always had breakfast together around the table and just talk and joke around. If I had a friend sleep over, they were always welcome and included, too," then you need to create this ritual *now*. For example, if you have a parenting partner, you would come together to create this family ritual of a weekly Sunday breakfast. Similarly, you would set the intention to have a welcoming household where your child's friends feel comfortable and like members of the family.

If you want your child to have a love of reading, now is the time to read to them regularly and let them see *you* reading for pleasure.

If you want your child to see you as a passionate entrepreneur who prioritizes their family, it's time to start reading the next chapter!

To finish this exercise:

- Write down a short statement of your True Vision, if you haven't already;
- Write down three to five things that you will do *now* to support this vision; and
- Schedule time to make it happen. Set up recurring appointments and reminders so that you follow through on the tasks and rituals that will support your vision.

⌛ **Fast Five:** Pick *one* thing that you want your future almost-adult child to say about you. This could be about how you made them feel celebrated, how you showed up in the ways that mattered most, or a family tradition that was important to them. Take a moment to write down what you will do *now* to create this future and when you will do it.

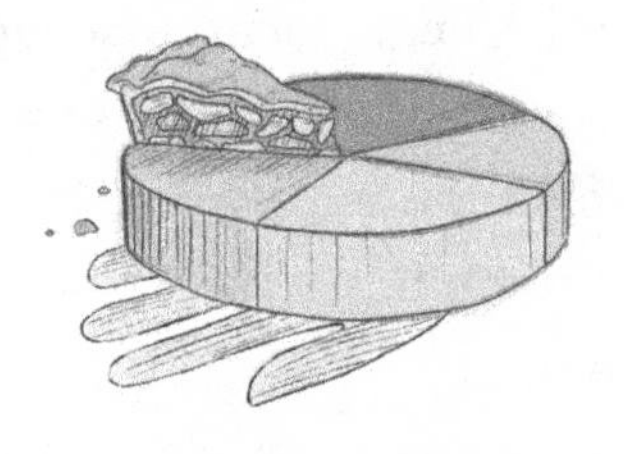

CHAPTER 5

AS YOUR CHILD GROWS, YOU CAN TOO

In our early homeschooling days, Alaina and I took my mom to an orthopedic doctor on a regular basis for an injury she sustained in a car accident. During these doctor visits, I was in "school mode." As Alaina and I sat side by side in the waiting room, crowded with older folks there for hip and knee replacement consultations, we attempted to do math and spelling worksheets. I was looking for every opportunity for efficiency and felt these minutes were the perfect time to get schoolwork done. It would be simple; she would sit there quietly and do her work while the TV played and this room full of strangers made small talk. I was basically repeating the same program and "disciplined" approach to her "learning" as she experienced in school.

Except there was a flaw in my plan: the doctor's office was a two-hour drive from our home, so Alaina had been cooped up long enough. She could not sit still, and she would not work on her worksheets. Getting her to focus on schoolwork when the room was full of potentially adoring fans was a wasted effort. She would rather work the room. I'm sure I looked like a tyrant and an idiot to that room full of more mature people. In my mind, I was supermom.

Thinking of that time now, I cringe. Granted, this was before I tuned in to how learning really works and how much better we all learn when it's fun. Still, it's hard to look back at that version of myself.

This was the first of many lessons I had learned about business but needed to translate into my mom role: When it comes to people, you strive for effectiveness, not efficiency. I knew the concept from Dr. Steven Covey's book, *The Seven Habits of Highly Effective People.*[15] I had applied it to many processes in my work life in the 1980s. But that day, I absorbed it on a deeper level. How could anyone learn in those conditions? Why had I set Alaina up for failure, all in the name of just getting it done? These little lessons learned as I tried to help my daughter put me on the path of self-development so that I could meet her where she was.

That lesson has stuck with me as I continue to develop my business. We measure efficiency, but understand that when we do, it's measuring processes, not people. This lesson in efficiency and effectiveness has played out over and over for me when I've tried to prioritize accomplishing a task expediently versus looking at the effectiveness of the end result and factoring in the people involved and the situations they face.

The time I attempted to develop an automatic client journey for our new clients is a good example of this. Our automatic client journey defines the path a lead will follow after they first express interest in our services and until they are onboarded as a client. The process allows us to filter their responses to ensure that we only talk to those people we can serve effectively. It is also designed to give new clients confidence that they are working with a competent organization. This is important because we typically have a two-month waiting period from the time someone signs our contract until we start their service. During this time, we want to eliminate any buyer's remorse by educating them and asking them for small bits of information. This keeps them engaged, yet not overwhelmed, as we assemble and prepare a packet for our onboarding team so they hit the ground running when it is time to start the project.

To get this process started in my business, I attended an online course, did the homework, shared my system with the workshop leader, refined and improved it, and was ready to hand it off to our internal business development team within a couple of months. As I turned it over to them, my internal dialog was, *Here it is. Plug it in and it will make your life easier and better.* I quickly learned at the handoff that the way I thought we did things was different from how we *really* did things. My team members' questions clearly showed that I had missed the mark. So much for efficiency when you must start over. Because the result was important, we did start over and the appropriate team members were involved in the process. The outcome was so much better. The system works, clients comment on it, and the team talks about time savings. They are clear on the process, roles, and responsibilities, and, best yet, they own the system. When something changes, they ensure that it still works and flows properly.

What we learn in one setting benefits us in another. What I first learned in business years ago when I was a devoted disciple of *The Seven Habits of Highly Effective People* (seriously, after I read it, I started a club at work to learn more about how my colleagues and I could incorporate these habits into our daily lives) benefited me in my personal life when I relearned it as my daughter's teacher. I recycled the lesson and relearned it for my business. I love how it all works together.

We're living a life! When we have children, it's to enrich our lives and theirs. When we start a business, it's to support our lives. When we grow in one area, we grow in all areas.

Now that you have gained clarity about your True Vision, you can start to design your life and business to support that vision. And as you and your child grow, your priorities will shift. New insights will inspire you to change your approach. Stay open and focused so you and your family can grow together.

LIFE PRIORITIES DRIVE BUSINESS GOALS

When you are a mom and a business owner, you have twice the number of decisions to make. The order in which you make these decisions matters. To make it all work, you need to determine your life priorities first. Here are a few questions to get the juices flowing:

- Do you prefer interacting with clients while providing a service, or would you prefer to create and market a product?
- Do you prefer to work alone or with a team?
- How much time will you work each week/day?

- When will you work?
- Will you work from home, or does it suit you better to go to another location?
- Will you have childcare? How will that impact your working hours?

I raise these questions to inspire you to consider what really works for you and how it can support your True Vision and your why. The rest of this chapter gives you options to consider based on my experience and the experiences of the many moms I interviewed. Even after you develop your plan, please, don't be married to it. It's never done; it's a process that will constantly change. As soon as you get it sorted out, the schedule will change. Naps and feeding, sports seasons, school, music lessons, etc., all are flexible, and you will learn that one of the few constants in your child's schedule is change. The exercises and the thought you put into them will help you to be nimbler.

FLEXIBILITY

I REALIZED EARLY ON THAT flexibility was going to be a huge priority for me as both a mom and a business owner. Between Alaina's tutors and her Tae Kwon Do schedule, things changed frequently, but I had made the decision from the get-go that Alaina's education was my priority, so I built my business to accommodate flexibility. I set the time I wanted to work. I set client expectations. I learned when I needed to be available to listen and do something fun and when she would like to do her own thing.

Once my daughter was school age, I thought I would consider a part-time job of some kind. Things changed when I realized that the kindergarten framework at the school and her teacher's style were not a good fit for Alaina's learning style. When she came home, she needed to have some alone time. She had to have time to process her day. As the school year progressed, I realized that her stress was real and very heavy. Each day, it took her two hours to decompress from school by playing alone to sort out or block out the day. I saw that it was taking a toll. In conversations with the teacher and a guidance counselor, Dave and I realized that the school in our rural area was not equipped to help.

Right before Valentine's Day of her kindergarten year, we made the decision to pull Alaina out of her school and homeschool instead. Luckily, I had the flexibility and the financial resources to make that happen. While I understand that not everyone can accommodate such a quick response, I have seen moms figure out plans that work for their unique situations over and over again.

Soon, my days were spent teaching, playing, and being the sole source of entertainment for my daughter. We both needed other interactions. Thankfully, our babysitter was also homeschooled, and she came over weekly to give me and Alaina a break from each other. I was very active in the local Master Gardeners group, and Alaina became my shadow and interacted with all the ladies, many of whom were grandmothers. She charmed them all.

Later, as Alaina needed more structured tutoring, we made the trips to her classes and I had two hours before lunch and two hours after lunch to fill. When I started my business, I used the hotspot on my phone to work in my car during these hours, or found a coffee shop or library I could work from.

As Alaina's tutoring progressed, her schedule expanded, and she began tae kwon do. At first it was an hour, but as her skills grew, the owner of the tae kwon do school offered her the opportunity to join the instructor training program. Our day started with a two-hour drive at around 8:00 a.m. She would be in tutoring from 10:00 a.m. to 12:00 p.m., and then we'd eat lunch and return to tutoring from 1:00 to 3:00 p.m. Then she was in tae kwon do from 3:30 until 9:30 p.m., when we would start the two-hour drive home. I basically had six hours to work while she was in tae kwon do. The working carrels at the library served me well. I spent two days a week at the library and used the library conference room to meet local clients. The productivity I experienced while Alaina was doing her thing was amazing.

Once I decided what was most important—my family and my daughter's education—the rest became logistics, just surmountable problems to solve. Knowing what to focus on and when I would have the time to focus made things much easier. In fact, flexibility and focus are the perfect combo in my world. There was time, when deciding on a core value of the business, that the team and I debated between "Flexible" and "Focus." Ultimately, the team's input helped us to decide on Flexible because our clients really appreciate our flexibility with their individual needs, and the team likes the flexibility in their schedules. I, however, find that focus and flexibility together are an incredible duo.

When Alaina decided to go to Brazil for the Rotary Youth Exchange program, my friend Nancy shared a great piece of advice with this cute phrase: "Blessed are the flexible, for they will never get bent out of shape!" How true this was for getting Alaina to Brazil, and for so many other things in life.

Getting clear on your priorities will help you make business decisions. Once you know your life priorities, they become another filter for your work decisions.

When you own a business, you must make choices as a matter of necessity. If you haven't given attention to your why, True Vision, and personal priorities, you'll be like a ship without an anchor, buffeted by a storm. You will be pushed and pulled by the forces in your personal and family life. The stress will be enormous, and you will constantly operate in a state of overwhelm. When you have an anchor, you will still be faced with the waves from the storm—and yet, when you see those waves coming, you will have a basis for how to respond. This will allow you to operate from a position of confidence.

One business advisor advised me to say no quickly. I love this approach and have found it so helpful. Too many times, I've delayed delivering a "no" response, and the longer I delayed the harder it became. I still had to say no, but my delay made it seem like I should have some major justification. A quick "No, this isn't a good time for me right now" takes it off your plate so you can devote your energy to your priorities.

As you make decisions about starting and growing your business, keep in mind the priorities and goals you have for your personal life. All these decisions—such as the type of work you will do, whom you will serve, what products or services you will sell, when or if to hire help, if you will work from home, etc.—need to align with your personal goals. For me, flexibility is an example of how my personal situation drove my business goals.

ALIGNMENT

ANOTHER STRATEGY FOR ENSURING THAT your business supports your personal goals is to align your type of work and customer base with your lifestyle. Of course, that's not possible if you're a brain surgeon or a builder, but for many service businesses, you can get really specific about for whom and with what and how you will work. As I developed my remote bookkeeping business, I was advised by my business coach, Mike Michalowicz, that I should specialize in an industry niche to ensure that my processes and systems could be developed and replicated.

The exercise Mike asked me to undertake was to look at my customer base and determine which types of customers I worked with the most. I had a web designer, a graphic designer, a digital marketing agency, a bicycle shop, a restaurant equipment business, and a few ecommerce businesses. All the non-ecommerce businesses were somewhat local to the area where my daughter was tutoring and taking tae kwon do. Occasionally, they would have issues with technology or software or just have a question they wanted to discuss. They would ask for a meeting and I'd pop in. I loved it, but it did require my presence.

The ecommerce businesses were all over the country. These business owners were very tech-savvy and operated entirely by selling on digital platforms like Amazon. They tracked their inventory on cloud software applications and bought their products through email communications with vendors all over the world. I liked that they were comfortable working from anywhere. Some of them characterized themselves as digital nomads and frequently moved from one tropical paradise to another because all they needed to work was a laptop and access to the internet. What they were doing intrigued me. I wanted to work with people who were tech-savvy and flexible so I could gain more flexibility in my own life. I was also a little envious of their adventures and hoped my business might one day afford that kind of travel/work arrangement.

As a result of this niche evaluation, I chose to work with ecommerce sellers because they aligned with what I needed and valued in my personal life. Ecommerce clients are typically after the same kind of lifestyle flexibility. They may have different motivations, such as our clients who are interested in world travel, but they are unconcerned with our availability between 8:00 a.m. and 5:00 p.m. and they don't expect us to drive to their offices for meetings, etc. They are comfortable with technology and outsourcing. Giving us admin access to their bank accounts and sales platforms does not scare them. They have people from all over the world helping them and they are fine with meeting online via video conference. These modes of operation are business as usual for them because they value flexibility, and we are in alignment on that life priority.

If I had continued to work with the "local" stores, I would have built a business that required more and more of my time in their presence. While I don't think an in-person presence is necessary, I still have many of those legacy clients and we never meet in person now; I believe my old approach would not have moved them into the virtual world. I would have continued to "pop in" because it's what I had always done. My mindset would have stayed in the mode of seeing them on occasion or when they needed me. As my business grew, that would have been a burden on my time and a limiting factor in my growth. By looking at what aligned best with my ultimate purpose, I found a niche that worked. Ultimately, it redefined my business in a way that I could not have imagined. Aligning with your priorities yields positive results. Consider them carefully and, once you decide, honor them.

After setting your life priorities and business goals for both, take it two steps further. First, determine what will be sacred in your home life. Then identify the immutable laws for your business. These important decisions will help to make your vision a reality.

SAVE YOUR SANITY: SACRED SPACE FOR FAMILY

WHAT ARE THOSE IMPORTANT TIMES or spaces that you will not let work invade? This boundary-setting exercise will help you train your mind to fully engage with your family. I will share many time management tips and strategies in the next chapter. For now, I'd like you to focus on what is important to you in everyday life.

You've already considered your life priorities, the big picture. Let's take an ideal day in your life: What would it look like? Do you want to sit down and get grounded with your child each morning over breakfast? Maybe you want to walk your child to school and walk them home? Perhaps you want your entire family together for dinner each night and for their sports events? Maybe you don't want to work in your family room, and you choose not to allow phones or computers there. What will make you and your family happy and truly together when you are together?

I didn't do a good job setting up these guidelines for my personal life when my daughter was young. I remember being tuned into my phone to keep up with the business during my time with Alaina. I allowed the dings from notifications to take me away from being fully present with her. I also recall allowing her to sit in my office when I was on calls, thinking she just wanted to be near me. In reality, I couldn't focus on my calls because she was actually there seeking attention. Looking back, and based on my interviews with moms for this book, I can see how setting boundaries for my work and family time would have saved me heartache and headaches!

Creating Sacred Space is vitally important and it's something that most mothers, especially mothers of only children, like me, struggle with. It is almost possible to raise one child without upsetting your entire world. However, small changes happen over time, and you find yourself feeling overwhelmed or unfulfilled. Using your support network and setting up accountability for yourself can help you win against that struggle. If you ignore it and operate under the illusion that you can take on one more "little" thing, you give up caring for yourself in the process.

> PROGRESS NUGGET: *"The greatest achievement was at first and for a time a dream. The oak sleeps in the acorn, the bird waits in the egg, and in the highest vision of the soul a waking angel stirs. Dreams are the seedlings of realities."—James Allen*[16]

SELF-CARE IS NOT OPTIONAL!

SELF-CARE ISN'T ABOUT FINDING TIME to take a bubble bath and read a book; it's about doing the hard work of eating right and exercising and saying *NO*. Self-care is not optional, so let's plan for it. Left to chance, something like this can happen: During Alaina's infancy, I started a downward spiral on days when I couldn't find time to take a shower. Not taking a shower one day had me feeling down, which made it harder to find time the next day and eventually, after three days, I would weep because I felt like I would never get to take another shower in my life. My can-do attitude was so far gone that all I could do was think about how it was never going to get better.

Fortunately, I had a great set of friends who wouldn't stand for this, and they gave me the support I needed. Maybe it was just sitting in my living room watching Alaina for a few minutes while I showered, or sharing an empathetic conversation about how my life and hopes and dreams were important too and I needed to find resources that gave me a break to work on myself and my dreams.

Don't leave this to chance. Great friends notice when you are overwhelmed, but you may relocate to a new area and distance makes those great friends less of a resource for you. Revisit the support list we discussed in Chapter 2 and ensure that you have someone on your team who is willing to watch out for you, hold you accountable, and step in to give you Sacred Space.

My neighbor Katie, for example, would pop in at such times with a spaghetti pie and say in her most caring way, "So, how are *YOU* doing?" She really wanted to know. She was also my lifeline to others who could help. At one point, the answer was teenagers she knew in the community. J'Lynn, Sarah, and Forrest were so much more interesting to Alaina than boring Mom. In addition, they were excited to contribute and loved having another adult to listen to how they viewed the world. I loved my time with those teenagers. It was always brief, as they were there to entertain Alaina and free me up, but it was fun seeing what was important to them.

Recently, I came across a friend's social media post in which she apologized to her two grown children for not always setting boundaries and appropriately modeling self-care. In this post, she shared an alternative ending to Shel Silverstein's book, *The Giving Tree*. You may recall the wonderful story of how a young boy befriends a tree that gives him so much happiness in his youth—apples to eat, branches to climb, and shade to nap under.

In the original story, as the boy grows into a young man, he visits his friend the Giving Tree and explains that he is too busy to climb trees and wants a house to keep him warm. His request is "Can you give me a house?" The tree is cut down for lumber and used to build a home for the boy's new family. The tree gives its life for him.[17]

I always thought this was such a sad story, and I cried every time I read it to my daughter. In the alternate ending by Topher Payne, the tree says, "Look, I was fine with giving you the apples to help you get on your feet. They'll grow back next season anyway.

"But no, I'm not giving you a house.

"You know, I've seen boys like you pull this nonsense with other trees in the forest.

"First it's the apples, then branches, then the trunk, and before you know it that mighty beautiful tree is just a sad little stump. Well, look here, Boy, I love you like family, but I am not going down like that."

The tree goes on to say that she has given to him year after year, but now he's too busy to visit and when he does show up, it's because he wants something. She gets his attention and teaches him that relationships work as a two-way street. In the end, the moral to the story is laid out clearly and plainly. "Setting healthy boundaries is a very important part of giving. It assures you'll always have something left to give. And so, the tree was happy. Everyone was."[18]

This alternate ending can help us envision a better relationship with our children that allows us to take care of ourselves.

AJ is a writer, as you may recall, and she shares how hard it is to manage these boundaries when it's your dream to make childhood ideal for your children. "I am a perfectionist. So it took me a really long time to learn how to balance and I didn't do a great job. It was really hard for me to meet deadlines because I really did put my child first and at the top, then my wife and me down at the bottom. I fell into a trap of not taking care of myself because I was so determined to do things differently from my parents."

AJ described her typical day. "Back when I was ghostwriting, my wife would take Jack to preschool. That meant that I had from eight to eleven in the morning to work, and then I would walk to pick him up. Even though I had a million things to do, because of this value, I took him to the park every single day. I had an Energizer bunny. He lit up there and he was so happy. I wanted him to have a sense of community and I wanted to be there for him. I wasn't one of those moms who had a laptop in my lap at the park."

As AJ explained in Chapter 1, all that focus on her child caused her to let other important aspects of her life slide. This caused a problem in her marriage.

"At the time, I had this myopic view. I thought, *I am focusing on the family. I'm bringing money in. That is what makes sense in my world.* I couldn't see my wife's point of view. I kept saying, 'I can't not work. The consequence of me not working is worse.' I kept saying, 'I have no choice.' And then I realized, *Well, actually, you could find time, you're just making a choice not to.* I had to have a sort of 'come to Jesus' moment with myself and realize that I was totally delusional. I was just believing my own hype."

AJ shares her story to show that while our goal may be to create a child-centric family, we can't ignore ourselves and other family members to focus solely on the child or children. Without boundaries, her health suffered as she gained one hundred pounds and her relationships with her wife, family, and friends also suffered. While her work flourished, she hadn't yet figured out how to better integrate work with family and childcare.

I also struggled with boundaries and work-life integration. It's so frustrating to work on a project only to be interrupted with, "Hey Mom!" At best, this is disruptive. The disruption can create anxiety around completing the work by deadline and anger about having so many demands on your time, and, without proper management, it can lead to working hours that rob you of time to care for yourself. Even as a teenager, Alaina would do her own thing; but when she had a few minutes, she would pop in my office and want to chat. The expectation was that I would drop what I was doing to visit for the time she had available.

I call this "kidnapping." Your kid has taken you hostage and you feel trapped, as if you were tied up and gagged and also the one who has to deliver the ransom in order to get free again. It's a troubling spot, and you need hostage negotiator training to secure your release. Our kidnappers use guilt and manipulation tactics with finesse and our desire to be close to them, to boost them up and create that child-centric family, puts us at a disadvantage. The way to escape is to remember what is sacred for you.

Tap back into your Sacred Space, where you connect with yourself and take care of you. Getting back on that solid foundation allows you to be your best self, which includes being an awesome parent to your child. If you find yourself repeatedly drifting away from your Sacred Space, then stop for a minute and set up some accountability for yourself. Check in with your support network and ask them for more structure in your relationship. If you don't have someone in your network to help with accountability, reach out to me at ApplePieMoms.com and I'll connect you with our free community. We'll find you a partner there.

IMMUTABLE LAWS FOR BUSINESS

NEXT, CONSIDER YOUR BUSINESS LIFE. In his first book, *The Toilet Paper Entrepreneur,* Mike Michalowicz explains what he calls "Immutable Laws." "You have certain hardwired beliefs that can't, won't, and shouldn't be changed. These beliefs are something we , and they continue to intensify over time. Not all of us share the same beliefs, and some of us have polar opposite beliefs. When recording the Immutable Laws for your company, they must be *your* personal values, not a watered-down version of what you think others want to hear… Remember, this is not about 'should,' this is about what is meaningful to you. So even if people are telling you that your Immutable Laws are impossible to adhere to or silly or useless, hang tight. When things get hairy or business booms or both, you'll realize how important those Immutable Laws are. Immutable Laws will keep you on track; you can draw strength from them in times of crisis and use them to help you make decisions fast."[19]

I have three Immutable Laws for my business. They are: "We will always be caring, grateful, and data-driven."

- **Caring**: "Respect for ourselves guides our morals; respect for others guides our manners." —Laurence Sterne [20]
- **Gratitude**: Gratitude helps us see what *is* there instead of what isn't.
- **Data-driven**: There is truth in the data.

When things are somehow hard and not flowing, it is usually because we have not paid attention to the data, failed to treat each other in a caring manner, or lost sight of what we have to be grateful for and started comparing ourselves to others. The shortcut to *not* landing in hard places is to follow your Immutable Laws. You will occasionally have to course-correct, but you will start from a position that aligns with who you are.

Recently, we were faced with a challenging client, Norm. Setting up his account took us much longer than we expected.

The delay was a combination of issues with our team and incomplete information from the client. For our part, we underestimated the complexity of his accounts during our proposal process and our onboarding process was in transition at the same time. We trudged along and finished the account, only to realize that the inventory component made no sense. We dug deeper. Our team was committed to delivering a good result.

Unfortunately, this was before our automatic client journey was in place, and we were not keeping Norm informed of our progress or delays. When a client has to ask about the status of their work, they already have doubts. We delivered the final product to Norm and he was pleased with the results of the project. At this point, he engaged us to clean up the prior two years' accounting. However, he took an opportunity to complain when we sent out our Net Promotor Score survey. He gave us a six out of ten.

We take this customer survey very seriously because the accounting industry average is an abysmal twenty-three. We currently have a score of seventy-two, which is in the World Class category. I called Norm to better understand his concerns and he requested a refund as the information was delayed. I took ownership for our part in the mess and shared that we were over budget by $2,000 and were not charging him for our poor budgeting. I reminded him of his non-responsiveness at times and how that contributed to the delays as well.

He was adamant and complained, "When we mess up with a client, we give a refund. Customer service is the most important rule in business!" Of course, his product cost was six dollars and we were over budget by $2,000. When his product is broken, it's unusable. Our product was far superior to any accounting work he had received before. He told us this when he engaged us to go back and clean up his books for prior years.

On the call, I told Norm, "We see the world differently, and perhaps we're not a good fit. I understand that you are unhappy, and in my experience, unhappy customers don't generally find their way to happiness." I was ready to walk away at that moment.

As he began to understand my position, he walked back his complaints and said, "I want to make this work. This is all in the past now. Let's start over with the monthly service." At this point, he had been receiving our monthly service for over a month and loved it. He raved about his bookkeeper, how great she was, and how smoothly things were going.

We agreed to give it another try. He was quiet for about two months, and then his annual contract renewal came up. During a call with Bree, our business development manager, she explained that his level of activity had increased significantly and the complexity of his account was requiring a lot more time. Here we were, negotiating again. I understand not wanting to pay for inferior work, but he clearly felt our work was superior to any he had received before. He griped and went away to think about it, then came back, agreed to our price, and wanted to add more work to our plate. We agreed and said that we would need to develop a price for the additional new work. As we quoted the new work, he picked apart the prior contract, which had a tiny "freebie" in it. Because he did not use this element of our service during the previous year, he wanted a refund. He knew we had served him for over a year at a price that was $2,000 below our standard rates, and yet he wanted a refund?

At that point, we withdrew our proposal and informed Norm that our work would end in thirty days as per the termination clause of the contract.

About two weeks later, he asked Bree, "Did Cyndi make this decision because I asked for a refund?"

We simply replied, "Your approach to our relationship was transactional, and we like to work in partnership." It's important to know your purpose and your boundaries because, while this entire situation was not fun, our decision was crystal clear.

Our Immutable Law of caring was stretched in the situation with Norm. We went out of our way to serve him, but his actions made it clear that he did not have the same values. I knew that my team would continually be confronted with challenging situations with this client and because I care for them, I chose to terminate the relationship with him.

Just as your Immutable Laws will help you make decisions within your business, knowing your purpose will help you make decisions that impact your family life. My purpose was ensuring my daughter's education. I could be flexible on most things, but getting her in front of the right tutors and set up with the right resources so she would value learning and reading was paramount for me. I wasn't so concerned with prestigious schools, but I was very concerned with critical thinking and her ability to achieve the things she may desire in life because she is so exceptionally brilliant. On that point, I wasn't flexible; I was focused.

With education for her as the focus, I was able to navigate flexibly through the other questions. I knew the strategy, and the rest, including every decision in my business, became a tactic that had to support that strategy.

Finding my purpose and letting it drive my other decisions has served me well over the years. My practice in almost everything I do is: Understand my why, focus on how to achieve it, and stay flexible with the rest of the details. Details can be managed once you know your destination. It's almost like having a compass and following the course—sometimes with precision and sometimes with an adventurous spirit. You let the important decisions guide your focus and then you can be flexible with the rest.

FOCUS POCUS

As a mom business owner, you will need extreme focus. When you get it and apply it, you make magic.

Your time must be used to achieve the most needed result for your family or for the business. That means you must go into "pop-up blocker" mode. You know, the setting on your internet browser that keeps all the distractions at bay. As the pop-up blocker for your life, your focus will serve as your filter, deciding what you pay attention to and what you decline or block. Even with focus, it ain't easy. The exercises you did for the last chapter were created to serve as pop-up blocker filters. How do you know what constitutes a distraction if you don't know why you do things or where you're trying to end up? If you skipped over those exercises, go back and give them the deep thinking they deserve. Everything you do going forward will be more obvious if you get clarity on your why and destination based on your learning from the exercises.

The best yardstick I have found to maintain focus on the important things comes from a book called *The One Thing* by

Gary Keller. In a nutshell, Keller suggests that we pick one thing and devote our attention to it. The question to help us decide is, "What is the *one* thing I can do, such that by doing it, everything else will be easier or unnecessary?"[21]

In a seminar I attended led by Geoff Woods, the co-founder of ProduKtive—the education company behind *The One Thing*—he taught the concept of geometric progression. Basically, this concept shows that small actions can have huge results. To illustrate the point, he used dominoes. A regular-size domino has the force to knock over a domino twice its size. If you extrapolate exponential growth, with just thirty-one dominoes, you could knock down the Eiffel Tower! It is amazing to consider that the small, consistent, focused actions you take can move you quickly toward your goals. The quote Geoff shared with us that I try to keep in mind is, "Think big, start small, trust the dominoes will fall."

Geoff's presentation was inspiring, and I have adopted the strategy of setting my one thing every day. Before I do anything else on my schedule, I accomplish the one thing that will make the next domino fall for me. First, I write for an hour. I know that putting words on a page for an hour every day is how this book will get completed. Spoiler alert: I finished the book!

In my weekly plan, I determine one to three big tasks for the week that will move my business forward. After I write, I work on these tasks first every day, moving them forward. Only when they are done do I look at the rest of the list. These tasks are my main mission for the week. By working in this manner, I can accomplish more in a year than I once dreamed possible. Think big, start small, trust the dominoes will fall! I've been doing it for three years, and it works!

CREATIVITY

After my daughter was born, one area where I experienced enormous growth was in my creativity. Maybe it was because, for the first time since I was fifteen years old, I was not working at a job. I was in a new location far from old friends and making new ones. I had made a new human; anything was possible after that!

During this time, I became an avid gardener, took art lessons and learned botanical drawing, and later learned pastels and painted. I learned about labyrinths and created a labyrinth of daffodils in a public park with my Arkansas Master Gardener group. I wrote a cookbook and started the work to create a children's museum in Hannibal, Missouri. It's kind of odd that when you're so tired and overwhelmed, you can also be creative. When I interviewed other moms, many shared a similar experience.

Laura, the Australian accountant mom, explained that she felt really creative after her boys were born. She attributed some part of her creative bursts to all the times when her mind was idle as she nursed or rocked her little boys to sleep.

Thinking about this from a business perspective, how much creativity do we bring to that part of our lives? I've found that when I'm very busy, I can't really step back and bring a creative bent to my problem-solving. Every problem looks like something to grind through and grunt out. When I make time in my schedule for "free time" or "thought time," I see the problems or opportunities through fresh eyes and the solutions are more inspired.

I build writing time into my schedule to ensure that my creativity stays in gear. This life "hack" has actually developed as I've written this book. For the last four months, I have dedicated the time between 9:00 a.m. and 10:00 a.m., every day, to join my writing buddies on Zoom. We mute ourselves and focus for two twenty-five-minute writing sprints. We chitchat for a couple minutes at the beginning and end, and during the halftime break we ask each other writing questions. As you might expect, this has been very productive from the standpoint of producing the book. What I've learned is that this focused creative time carries through for the rest of the day. My attention is more easily focused on my work tasks, whatever they may be. I am also "in gear" when it comes to creative problem-solving. It's like my writing time stretches my creative muscle and it is primed and ready for use all day.

How did I discover this? Because I set my priorities for my life. I realized that I wanted to write this book and I made time in my schedule to focus on it. Taking these steps helped me see that I can build time for creativity into my business life. It doesn't have to be left to chance or based on a child's nursing schedule. Don't overschedule yourself or allow your attention to be pulled into busywork. Do schedule yourself for creative work. It will connect your entire day to creative inspiration.

If, reading this, you're at the point of not knowing when you'll get a shower today, I know that creativity may sound like an idea too luxurious to entertain. However, just like self-care, it's not optional. When you start to ignore your needs, whether they are physical, emotional, or spiritual, you lose touch with who you are. I heard this from the moms I interviewed, and I have experienced it myself. When I was a full-time, stay-at-home mom before I started my business, and after my daughter was grown and I gave my business nonstop attention, I reached the point of wondering, *Who am I?* When you get to this place, you're burned out and having an identity crisis.

WHEN YOU LOSE YOURSELF

IDENTITY IS TIED UP WITH our vocation, and both parenting and being a business owner can require such a level of immersion that you no longer know who you are. Getting in touch with your purpose helps you navigate these demands on your time and attention.

There were two times in my life when I felt I had lost touch with who I am. The first was when Alaina was an infant and my life was feeding and diapers, not sleeping and not showering. I'm not sure I knew what day it was, let alone why I was alive on this planet. The second time was when my business was growing and I couldn't keep up. I worked all day and half the night. Eating and sleeping were my only diversions from work. All the things I loved, like my garden and my animals, were cared for at only subsistence levels. I recall looking out the window of my office one day when the weather was perfect and I couldn't go outside to work in the dirt, deadhead the flowers, and weed. The flower beds were overgrown and I couldn't see past what wasn't getting done. Tears streamed down my face. What was I working for? The only thing I could see in my future was more work.

Both situations came from not having balance in my life. Early on, my family life did not afford me any time to embrace the vocational and creative side of my brain. Years later, my work life took all my time and energy away from my family and the fun aspects of life. Don't get me wrong, I'm not a big proponent of work-life balance. I don't think there are many occasions when the scale isn't tipped toward one side or the other. Pursuing balance is like pursuing perfection. You might achieve it for a day or a week, but it never lasts. I do think we can integrate our families and our work and achieve alignment of purpose, which allows us to set priorities and have the flexibility to shift our focus as the demands of family and work dictate. Having support networks and backup plans for family and work also allows us to better navigate these waters.

Julia, whom we met in the last chapter, was on maternity leave with her second child, Wilder, as she initiated her ecommerce business. When her maternity leave was over, she returned to her position as an online communications specialist and tried to negotiate for a part-time position. When that didn't work out, she left her job to fully launch her ecommerce business. Julia describes her time at home with Wilder and her first child, Josephine (JoJo).

"Wilder would take naps and was a pretty content baby, too. I could put him down and he wouldn't scream, which is not something I was used to with JoJo. I was able to get quite a bit done until he was a year to fifteen months, maybe, and really was not napping as much. He was up and walking and getting into everything. There was definitely a period of struggle there. When he was two, he started going to daycare four days a week. At first, I was really nervous and four days was way more than I wanted. It ended up being really good. I dropped JoJo off at her first day of kindergarten and Wilder off at his first day of daycare on the same day.

"We were totally ready for it. Because JoJo had done preschool, she was good to go. I was excited for her. I wasn't the crying mom at kindergarten. Next, I dropped Wilder off and I walked back and I sat down at home and it was suddenly like, *I can breathe.* Oh, it was like not realizing you had been drowning for the last year. And then suddenly being pulled out of the water. And I realized, *This is actually really good. This is the right time for this, too, for the little ones to be getting socialization. And for me to focus more on my business and myself, and be able to move on.*"

It's an unsettling feeling when you don't know who you are, when you say to yourself, *Why am I doing this? Why does this even matter?* And when you can't see yourself in a different situation in the future. If you get to this point, or when you do, step back, take a few deep breaths, and realize your purpose. Call on that support network and get away for a few days. In their TED Talk entitled "The cure for burnout (hint: it isn't self-care)," Emily Nagoski and Amelia Nagoski share that "What you need is a bubble of love around you. People who care about your well-being as much as you care about theirs. Someone to say, 'You need a break. I'm going to help you with this. I'm going to step in in that way.'"[22] When you reconnect with your purpose, you can start to evaluate your everyday reality and deal with the chronic stressors.

While the overwhelm, stress, and loss of connection with anything that matters may feel insurmountable, they are just other problems to solve and, as a parent and an entrepreneur, this is where you excel. You must take action to grow past this point. A quote from Henry Ford that I love is, "Whether you believe you can do a thing or not, you are right."[23] Make or take the time to think, and you can resolve this problem and get back in touch with what your purpose in life and business truly is. The answer is getting in touch with your purpose and using it to filter all activity. Use your network so you can protect your Sacred Space and focus on what is important. Disregard the busywork and let creativity flow.

These places where we're uncomfortable are where we grow—hence the phrase, "Get comfortable with the uncomfortable." I personally hate the idea of being uncomfortable, but I love the idea of learning, growth, and change. I can wrap my head around pursuing something much more easily than enduring something. Pushing through an identity crisis, setting aside your Sacred Space, creating focus and flow in your life as you set and pursue priorities—these are huge growth opportunities.

GROWING TOGETHER

MY FRIEND TRACY OWNS AN accounting practice in Phoenix, Arizona. Tracy learned from her son Lance's teacher that he needed assistance with executive functioning. As she understood his challenges, she realized that she too needed assistance in this area. Tracy describes her journey with her coach:

"It's basically like time management, goal setting, breaking things down into steps. Executive functioning is buying the birthday present the day before instead of buying it at Target on the way to the birthday party kind of thing. You know, having Lance and seeing how he's wired has made me recognize certain things in myself. Executive functioning is one of those things that I recognized where I need a little bit of support. I have been seeing an executive functioning coach to help with putting things on the calendar, breaking things out into smaller chunks, blocking out time for things, recognizing how long certain things are going to take so I block out an appropriate amount of time to work on them, that kind of stuff.

"When the teacher told us that he struggles with this and that's not a typical thing to struggle with, I realized, *Well, I struggle with it.* I asked the teacher, 'What do you mean it's not normal? It's my normal.' But to move forward, I told her, 'I guess most people don't have this particular struggle, so let's see how we can figure it out together.' Clearly, I don't have the skills to teach him this, so why don't I get some skills and then I can learn for myself and also help him."

I love how Tracy rolls up her sleeves and is willing to learn to help Lance and to improve herself. I'm sure this will help her in her business. This story illustrates my final point. While you grow your family and your business, the real growth occurs in you, which then allows all the other aspects of your life to grow as well. Continue to be flexible while you pursue growth and integration. When things are out of kilter, step back and reflect a moment. Then you'll know exactly how to dig in.

I always loved how Pop and my grandmother grew old together. They were married for over seventy years. But as I think back, they weren't just growing old together, they were always growing together. Grandmother taught Pop how to read at the dinner table when he was in his fifties. Every year they experimented with different flowers in the garden and making different types of jellies and jams. Growing old together is romanticized in our culture, but growth doesn't need to wait until you're old. Instill that learning in your children by being a learner. Maintain sacred time and boundaries, and your child will learn that, too. You'll also attract and retain clients who appreciate the same values. When you take time to do the exercises that follow, you are taking the steps to grow together with your child(ren). This miraculously makes managing your time each day and each week easier.

YOUR IMMUTABLE LAWS

Suggested Time to Complete: Twenty minutes.

When you complete this exercise, you will have a set of basic, enduring principles upon which you will build and grow your business.

If you skip this exercise, you sail away from the dock without a rudder or compass. You won't have a set of principles to guide you and your employees in making decisions, whether they be easy or challenging.

Your Immutable Laws for your business are those basic principles that you will not compromise. Once you develop them, they will be like *gravity:* an ever-present, nonnegotiable force. Your Immutable Laws will drive your decision-making, whether the decision is an easy one (like getting out of bed—you don't think much about gravity) or a complex one (like launching a rocket, where gravity plays a central role).

As you plan for your business, you will want to set your Immutable Laws early on. Doing so will help guide you in the early days as your business takes shape.

Begin crafting your Immutable Laws *now*. You can begin to work on these when you have a few minutes of quiet time. You'll need twenty to thirty minutes to complete the exercise below. There are some questions to help kickstart your flow, but don't feel limited by them! If you feel stuck, just let your subconscious work on them for a few days and you'll find that odd memories arise or references appear that help you get your head around them. Take notes so you don't lose these ideas. When you sit down to look at them again, they will make more sense.

Let's dive in!

Your Clients

- Think of times when you paid for a service or product and had a truly exceptional experience. What made these experiences exceptional?
- What types of clients do you want to work with? It may be tempting to say "ones that pay on time," but really think about who *you* want to work with. Describe them.

Your Employees

- In your past positions, what did you take pride in? What did you like about the company or leadership? What did you dislike?
- You are, presumably, starting a business so that you can live a lifestyle different from your current one. Will your business empower employees to do the same?

- What characteristics will be most important to you when hiring employees? (Answer this question even if you *think* you don't plan to hire anyone.)

Your Community

- Who comprises your business's community? This could be a description of your client/customer set, a local community, or both.
- How will you serve your community?
- How will you give back to your community?

Now, review your answers. Underline or highlight common words or themes in your answers in all three areas. Which ideas are keystones for you? Take these and craft your Immutable Laws. Once you have finalized your Immutable Laws, keep them somewhere where you will encounter them every day. For example, you may decide to print them and hang them in your office, include them in your desktop background, or inscribe them in your planner.

If you're feeling a bit stuck, here are examples of the Immutable Laws of some of the businesses featured in this book:

- People are more important than work.
- Craft beats talent, and you can learn craft.
- We best our best.
- "No" to toxic positivity but "yes!" to seeing the positives in each opportunity.
- Kindness and compassion are mandatory.
- No bullshit tolerated.

⌛ **Fast Five:** While it's never too late to create a set of Immutable Laws, your business will function and grow better when they are in place from the beginning. So, you *will* want to revisit the full exercise in the future.

If you are short on time now, spend five minutes zeroing in on your why. Answer these questions:

- Why are you reading this book? Why do you want to start a business? How will you craft your business in a way that supports those desires?
- Why will customers come to you? What will be unique about your business?

PROGRESS NUGGET: *Phew, you're more than half way through the book! If you can read just ten pages a day, you'll finish this book in nine more days.*

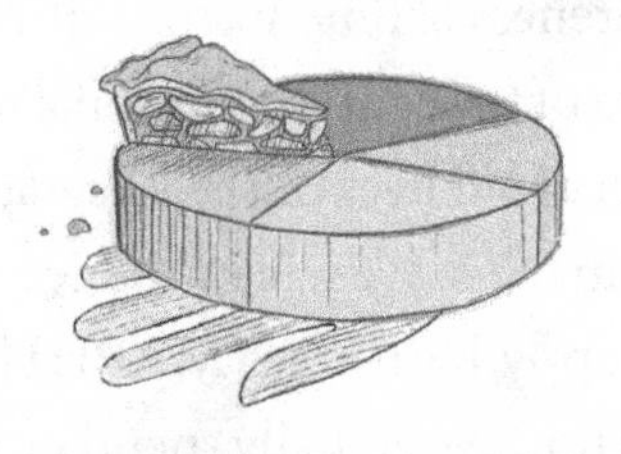

CHAPTER 6

MAKE TIME TO PUT YOUR DREAMS FIRST

It's time. Time to put your dreams first. To do this, you must manage your only finite resource: time. You can make more money; you can use that money to amplify your ability to get things done. But we all start with twenty-four hours in a day. How will you use yours?

In this chapter, we'll begin with the big picture and get real about the time you have left (possibly, if all goes as planned) to build your dream life. With that perspective in mind, realize that time management is not a rigid, do-every-day-the-same type of "system." We'll look at our priorities and how they change from day to day, sometimes even hour by hour. This approach will help us recognize that some balls are glass and shouldn't be dropped, while others are rubber and can easily bounce over to tomorrow.

With a new awareness of time and priorities, we will begin to understand our use of time for our personal needs and growth and how that aspect of our lives can be integrated with our mom and businesswoman roles. We will introduce the Motherhood, Apple Pie, and Happy Horsehit (MAPHH) Framework to begin considering how we actually spend our days, compared to how we'd like to. Inevitably, armed with information about this, we decide we want to make a change.

In the last two sections of this chapter, we will dive into two tools—Time Blocking and Accountability Partners—that work together to make sure you schedule and complete the items that are important to you. By doing the important tasks, you will ensure that you build your whole life in an integrated way so that you make your dreams come true by putting them first.

As you can see, there is lots to accomplish in this chapter, and we aren't getting any younger! So let's start our journey by looking at the big picture and getting real about your time.

REAL TIME

Our first step is to consider how many weeks you have left on this Earth. An ecommerce colleague, Steven Black of Unstoppable Marketing Masterclass, shared this image on his Facebook page.

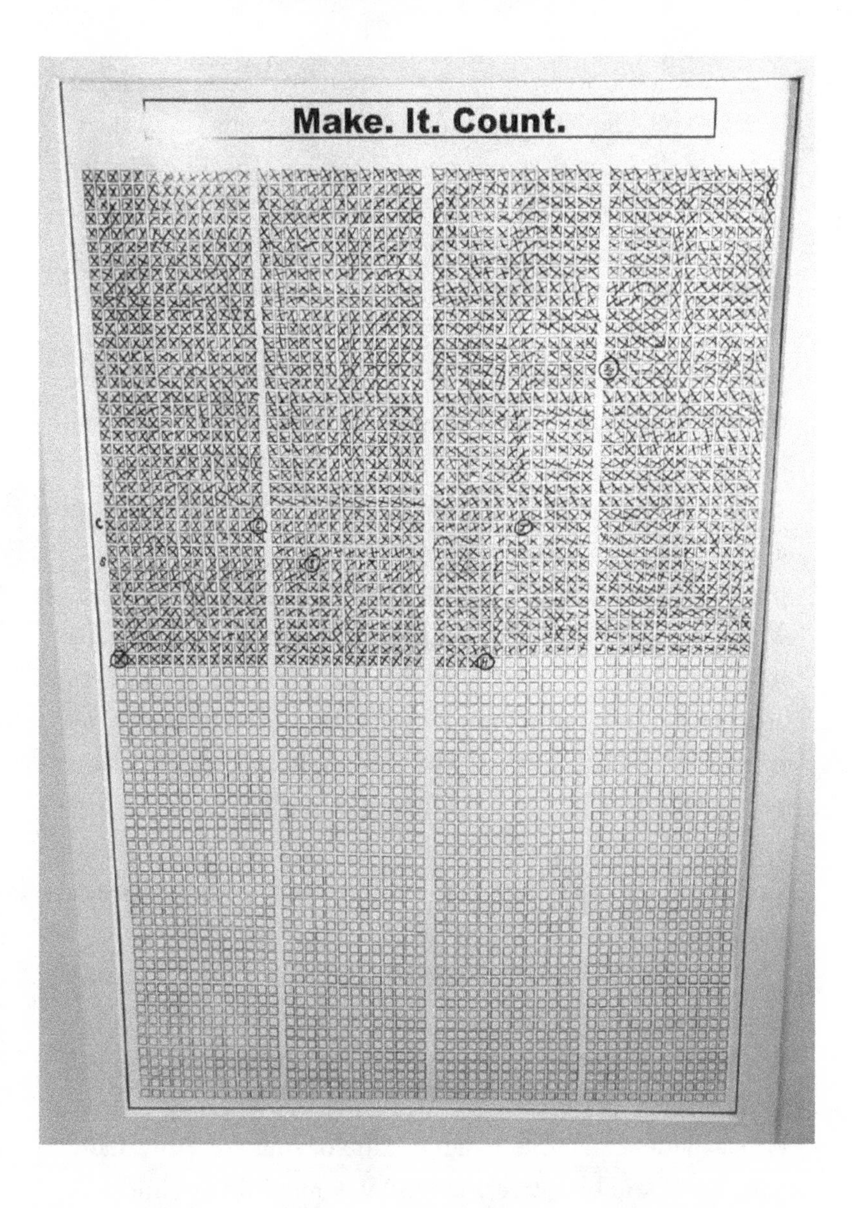

This chart represents all the weeks Steven has lived and expects to live. Wow! He's looking at his entire life span! At the end of each week, Steven determines whether he did, in fact, live his life with intent during the previous seven days. If he didn't, he makes a note with the reason. If he did, he checks the box with a flourish. The knowledge that he will face marking the box at the end of the week spurs him to show up and live life on his terms. What motivates Steven is his desire to look at his life's story during his last thirty seconds on Earth and say with certainty, "I did that on purpose. I did everything I could to leave humanity in a better place than where I found it."

Steven shared with me that he had a bout of depression after a couple of business failures that left him in a very dark place. A fellow entrepreneur gave him *Profit First* by Mike Michalowicz,[24] and it reached Steven deep inside and gave him hope. Now, he uses the method in his current businesses and teaches it to his ecommerce clients. Steven is one of the most driven human beings I've met, and the quality and quantity of the content he shares in his group is unparalleled. His approach to making each moment count is truly an expression of Sacred Space and is something each of us can do for ourselves.

How many weeks would you say you have left to live? I know we don't really know, but we're making plans here, and it helps to visualize a time span. If you are thirty years old and expect to live eighty years, you can easily see that you may already have experienced more than one-third of your life. How many weeks will you be actively parenting your child or children? Depending on how many children you have, there goes another third of your life.[25]

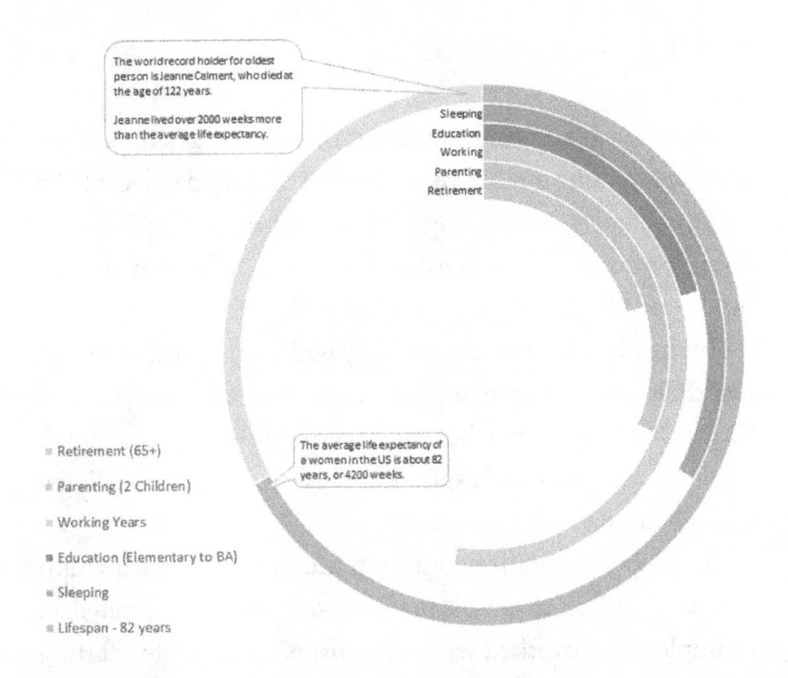

My point here is twofold. One, time goes by in a hurry because it is so busy. Two, you don't want to spend the next twenty to thirty years putting off your passion until your parenting days are over. You will be delaying your purpose in life until you're past the halfway point. Now, I'm definitely a late bloomer in this scenario, and I wouldn't really change a thing. However, if I had thought about my life in this way sooner, I might have been more tuned into its speed and made more ambitious choices earlier.

PROGRESS NUGGET: *May 14 is National Apple Pie Day in the United States. What do you want to be different about your life by Apple Pie Day?*

YOUR LIFE IN WEEKS

YOU OFTEN HEAR CHILD-REARING DESCRIBED as a time when the days are long but the years are short. Every day seems like a slog of diapers and fighting naps. Later, it's shuttling between dance and sports practices and trying to help with algebra homework.

In the blink of an eye, your baby will be grown. But it's not just their growing up that goes by in a flash; it's *your* life, too. So it's vital that, during the long days of mothering, you attend to your own needs and aspirations as well. It is *your* life flying by, right along with your child's.

To help you picture your own life in weeks, use a graph similar to Steven's from the previous section. I have created an example chart overlaid with dates from my own life, starting at age eighteen:

a. Age eighteen, started first "real" job as receptionist
b. Age twenty, married David
c. Age thirty-four, graduated from university
d. Age thirty-five, left North Carolina and corporate career as Vice President of Business Development to move to Missouri and start family
e. Age thirty-six, daughter Alaina born; active volunteer
f. Age forty, moved to North Central Arkansas; active volunteer and homeschool mom
g. Age forty-nine, began consulting to help a friend
h. Age fifty-one, founded bookskeep
i. Age fifty-five, published first book, *Profit First for Ecommerce Sellers*

LIFE IN WEEKS *of* CYNDI THOMASON

Ages 15-75

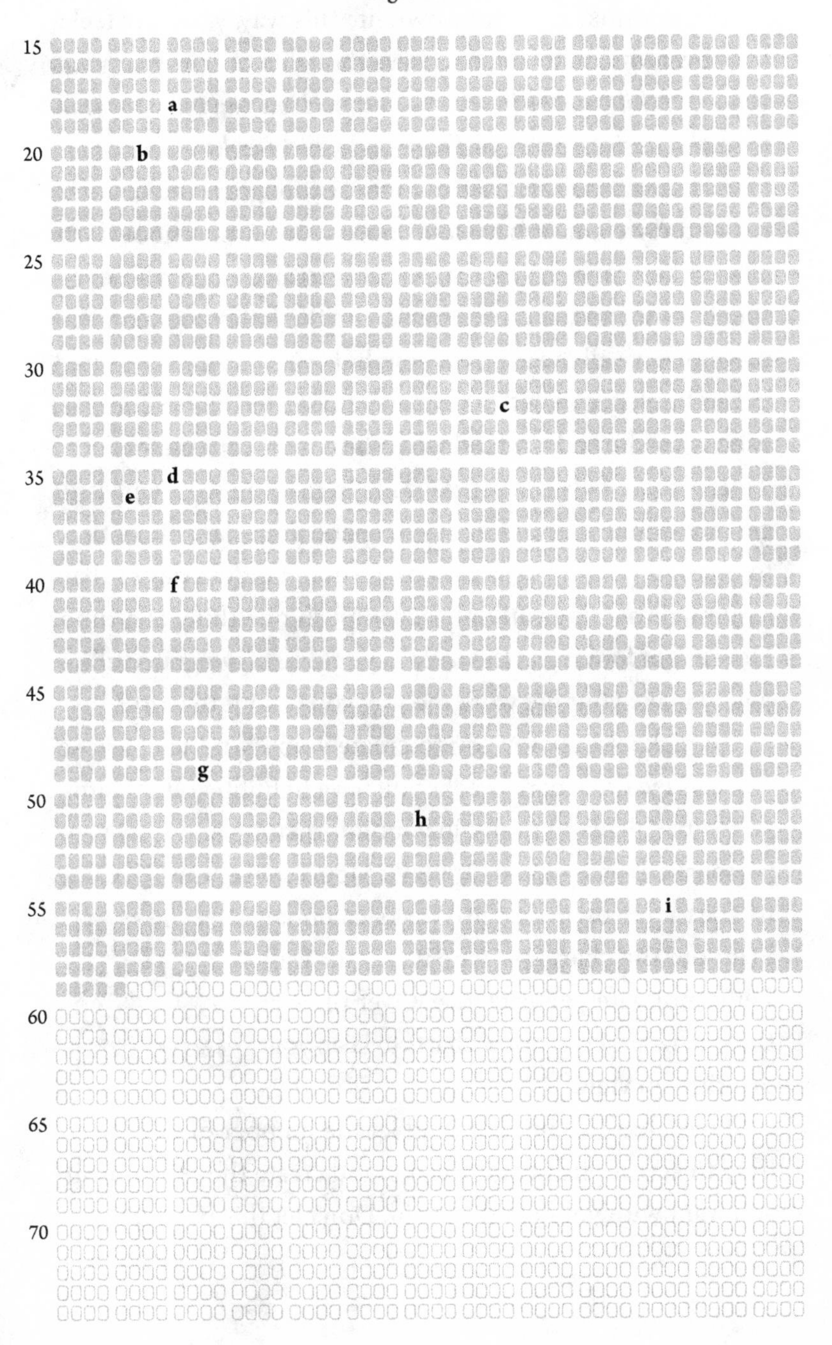

While thinking of your own life this way, you may feel a little overwhelmed. You may have thoughts like, *It's four years before my child will be in school full-time. How can I find the time to start a business now?* or *I'm already thirty-eight—I'm too old to start something new!* Let go of those thoughts. You're going to be thirty-eight or have four more years until school starts *anyway.* You can't change that. What you can change is how you spend tomorrow, and next week, and the following year. You may not have all the answers now, but every business featured in this book began with a woman who started where she was, used what she had, and did what she could. You can too.

The goal of visualizing your life in discrete segments is to get you thinking about how you spend your days. Take time to consider what you can accomplish in tandem rather than assuming that you can only accomplish one thing at a time. How might looking at the roles in your life as integrated allow you to make your life work the way you want it to work?

To make it easy for you to create your own life chart, so you can see how many weeks you have to fulfill your dreams, go to our calculator to put in your information and view your personalized chart. Go to ApplePieMoms.com or the QR Code to start your own Life in Weeks calendar. Print out the chart and tape it to your wall. Let it motivate you each day. Over time, as things change, create new charts to keep your priorities in view.

Take a look at the chart and let the number of weeks you have to accomplish your dreams, and create the relationship you want with your child, sink in. Don't let this paralyze you;

instead, let it energize you and encourage you to make the most of your time.

With this awareness in mind, let's look at all the important balls you are juggling. As we think about our priorities, we can ensure that our weeks stack up to create the life we want.

JUGGLING GLASS BALLS AND RUBBER BALLS

BRIAN DYSON, A FORMER CEO of Coca-Cola, gave a commencement speech in 1991 that adds perspective to our time-related issues. "I would caution you that as intelligent and active participants in a dynamic society like America, you must bring balance into your lives. Imagine life as a game in which you are juggling some five balls in the air. You name them—work, family, health, friends and spirit—and you're keeping all of these in the air. You will soon understand that work is a rubber ball. If you drop it, it will bounce back. But the other four balls—family, health, friends and spirit—are made of glass. If you drop one of these, they will be irrevocably scuffed, marked, nicked, damaged or even shattered. They will never be the same. You must understand that and strive for balance in your life."[26]

As I have mentioned before, I don't believe in work-life balance; but I strive to integrate work and other aspects of my life. This concept that not all balls are glass is interesting to ponder, and I like to take the analogy a bit further. Instead of five balls, let's imagine five baskets where we put our balls. Borrowing from Brian, we can name our baskets Family, Health, Friends, Spirit, and Work, but you may have other names or a different number of baskets. Then, let's be honest with what we're juggling; there are a lot more than five balls.

When I talked with Julia, she described it like this: "All these things I'm juggling aren't just work and kids and marriage/relationship and self-care; it's not just four balls. It's the individual, tiny balls of my Pilates class, and my kid's school play, and this kid's soccer practice, and the soccer game, dinner tonight, and making lunch for them. You have to decide: What are the ones that you can drop and they'll just bounce, and what are the ones that are going to shatter? You must cut some of it out especially in this world where we're just always bombarded with images of overachievement and perfection. Maybe your kid doesn't have the perfect bento box lunch with the flower-shaped cucumbers. That's okay. They can have school lunch. You have to make your choices considering all the balls, and not expect them all to be of the same importance all the time."

Julia makes it real. And I totally agree: life isn't as simple as juggling the broad areas of family, health, friends, spirit, and work. As a mom and a business owner, you probably have thirty, or fifty, or a hundred and fifty different balls to juggle on a given day. Now consider the makeup of these balls: How many are glass and how many are rubber this week, or today? And realize, the substance of these balls may change over time; this week, the ball to check in with your mom's doctor is rubber, but next week, she has developed a nasty cough. Since your mom is prone to pneumonia, the ball has turned to glass. Let's use this framework and evaluate each of the balls regularly to ensure that we don't drop the glass ones.

Knowing which upcoming tasks are represented as glass balls and which are rubber, plan ahead to take special care of the glass balls. Get comfortable with being human and knowing that you can't snap your fingers and accomplish things instantly (which means not overscheduling your time). And, to Julia's point, give up on overachievement and perfection. They aren't real life. Learn the patterns that appear with your glass and rubber balls. Based on those patterns, you can develop rhythms that work for you and your family and integrate your mom and business roles.

PROGRESS NUGGET: *"Don't count the days, make the days count."—Muhammad Ali*[27]

EXAMINING YOUR LIFE AND TIME USING THE MOTHERHOOD, APPLE PIE, AND HAPPY HORSESHIT FRAMEWORK

Most of us don't really know how we spend our time. It's common for moms to wonder, *What did I do all day?* as they get ready for bed. This happens in business, too. Your vision is blurry from working on your computer for six hours and yet you can't really name what you accomplished. To create the life we want, though, we have to be intentional. To understand what we might want to change, we have to realize our starting point. It is not enough to remember what we did most recently or what was the most painful or enjoyable, we must ensure that we have good baseline data.

Let's get a more holistic picture of your time as an entrepreneur crafting a business around your role as a parent. If you look at how you spend your days, you will likely find that your time is spent:

1. In service to your family;
2. In service to your business or career; and
3. In service to yourself.

From these three broad areas, it's useful to break your time down into the eight categories that make up the Motherhood, Apple Pie, and Happy Horseshit Framework. Each category is described below. Reflecting upon and eventually auditing your time according to these eight categories will help you better understand how you're using your time and what you need to do to use it in more fulfilling and productive ways:

Motherhood—Time in Service to Your Family

Mothering—This is time spent teaching and nurturing your child(ren). It encompasses everything from feeding and diapering your newborn to helping your fifth-grader with fractions to cheering on your child's team on game day.

Partnership—This is time you spend with your spouse or romantic partner *as partners*. Hopefully, if you have a partner, they are your biggest cheerleader and champion, and you have shared goals for your family. Find *quality* time to spend with your partner, honoring your relationship.

Family Management—This is time spent on the tasks that keep your family running. It includes planning and executing activities like meal planning and preparation, scheduling and attending medical appointments, maintaining the family calendar, and coordinating childcare.

Apple Pie—Time Spent in Service to Your Business

Business Management—This time will evolve with your journey as an entrepreneur. As you start out, you'll probably be the one responsible for most, if not all, of the functions of your business. It's like you're on a tiny sailboat, with just one sail and a rudder, and you're focused on making it to the next buoy. As you grow, you will need to look more closely at these tasks to see what actions can be delegated to your employees or consultants. You'll be the captain of a larger ship then, and you'll want to make sure your focus is on setting the course of your journey, not swabbing the deck.

Business Design—Where "Business Management" is about getting *it* done, the time spent designing your business is time when you envision and shape its future. This is how you figure out how your business will grow *and* stay true to your goals and vision.

Happy Horseshit—Time Spent in Service to Yourself

Oxygen—This is time spent on self-care and rest. To achieve your goals, *you* have to take care of *you*. Much as flight attendants instruct you to put on your own oxygen mask before assisting others, you'll need to make self-care and rest a priority. Without it, all your other activities will be harder and feel less meaningful. Self-care activities and rest nourish your mind and body in positive ways and improve your sense of well-being. Outside of the newborn time bubble, where everything can get rather cattywampus, self-care is *not* attending to your basic hygiene and nutritional needs. Don't settle for a shower, a balanced meal, and sleep for your self-care. Those are basic human needs; self-care addresses your higher-level needs.

Sacred Space—This is time in which you connect with your deep desires and truths, time when the answers to life's big questions come to you. Sacred Space is a very personal experience. You may find it while gardening, running, or journaling, or during another activity or restful moment. While you may find yourself in Sacred Space during a self-care activity, Sacred Space is really a state unto itself. If during activities such as exercising or a nice hot bath, you continue to worry over your concerns and attempt to solve them, you have not entered Sacred Space. Sacred Space occurs when you lose track of time and worries and are almost unaware of your thoughts. What feels like being lost in thought is really connecting to your deepest self.

Time Spent in Disservice

Distracted Disservice—This fourth category is a bit of a "negative bonus," but it must be acknowledged: Distraction is something we all turn to at times. Time spent on distracted disservice is time spent on unproductive activities that are neither nourishing nor restful. This could be time spent scrolling through social media in a mindless way, or on an "important" activity that doesn't really move the ball forward. These activities can look different for different people. For example, one mom may find being president of the PTA a fulfilling use of their energy and time, while another may consider it a dreaded obligation. The latter has created a distraction that keeps them from engaging with more meaningful activities.

We often turn to distraction—in both our personal and professional lives—when we are experiencing negative emotions like frustration, fear, or confusion. Maybe you've had a frustrating day with your overtired toddler and turn to social media for the little spike in dopamine it provides. Perhaps you're facing a difficult but critical task necessary for your budding business and turn instead to tweaking your logo or finding the perfect color palette for your website. You've filled your time, but you didn't move the ball forward in a meaningful way *and* you didn't derive fulfillment or happiness from the time spent.

DIVIDING YOUR TIME

WITH THE MAPHH FRAMEWORK IN place, you can categorize your time and examine how you're spending your days and weeks. But what does the ideal day or week look like? What should the targets be for each area?

The answer will depend on *you*. Here's an example of what the breakdown of a mom business owner's week might look like:

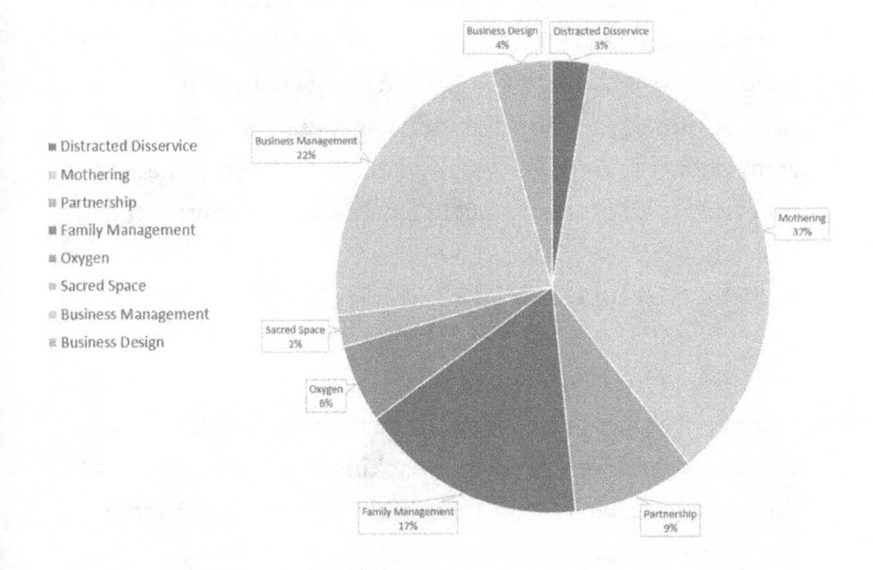

Looking at this example, we can imagine that this woman has young, school-aged children who go to a public school on a normal schedule. She spends 37 percent of her time on Mothering tasks before school and in the afternoons and evenings after school. A mom with a baby who is not in daycare would probably spend a larger percentage of her day on Mothering, and a mom with high-schoolers may spend less. Our fictional mom swims twice a week and either goes for a walk or spends time in her garden each day for Oxygen. While this is a relatively low percentage of her time, it's rejuvenating and feels good. She is feeling some frustration around the more tedious Family Management chores and the time they take up; maybe she can take back some time by combining her twice-a-week grocery trips into a single one, or having her kids take on some age-appropriate chores.

Examining how you spend your time within this framework, you can understand where things are out of balance and need to be addressed. It allows you to go from the overwhelm of "I never have any time!" to "Yikes, I'm spending four hours a day staring at my phone! I should be able to cut that in half and make some time for that daily walk I want to incorporate into my routine."

WHAT ABOUT MULTITASKING?

You have probably heard people say that moms are the ultimate multitaskers. Let's not listen to those people! Though you can scramble eggs while packing a school lunch and directing your kids to get their backpacks ready for school, our brains are not good at multitasking. Often when you think you're multitasking, you're just rapidly switching between tasks. The tasks you split your attention between can end up taking longer than they would if you maintained a singular focus, and the output may be of lower quality. Constantly splitting your focus can also make you feel frustrated, overwhelmed, and anxious.

If you seek to multitask, you need to be reasonable in your choices and expectations. Only engage in multitasking if you can do so while keeping your focus *nearly* singular. For example, I can effectively listen to an audiobook while I'm folding laundry. It's effective because:

1. Most of my attention is on the narrator's voice while my hands do the folding;
2. There's only one auditory input (the audiobook) and one physical input (folding); and
3. I'm combining a task I don't like (folding) with one that I do (learning).

Lastly, the consequences of a poor result are negligible. I can backtrack in the audiobook if I miss something, and it really doesn't matter if the folding is sloppy.

But what if the tasks demand equal attention or suddenly shift from mindless to complicated? If you've ever turned down the radio in the car when you took a wrong turn or traffic picked up, you already know the answer: You need to remove some of the inputs so you can focus. The same is true of any task that requires your focus. If, for example, you try to email a client while helping your child with their math homework, you set both yourself and your child up for frustration. She interrupts with questions, you lose your train of thought—and perhaps, eventually, your temper—and suddenly you are both having a very negative experience.

When it comes to your time, focus on the quality of your experience and outputs. There will be times that feel overwhelming and when there are many high-focus tasks on your plate. Rather than turn to ineffective multitasking, go back, ask which of the tasks are glass balls and which are rubber, and check in with your values and Immutable Laws. Remember that perfection is generally impossible, but progress is always possible.

MASTERING YOUR TIME IN THREE EXERCISES

TAKING CONTROL OF YOUR TIME is an ongoing process. The first two exercises below are quick but meaningful and effective ways to begin this process. The third exercise is more involved but will enable you to take an in-depth, critical look at your days.

EXERCISE 1: WEEKLY REFLECTION

- **Suggested Time to Complete:** Twenty minutes, spread out over one week.

- **When you complete this exercise,** you take the first step toward better time management. Knowing the reality you're living now is the first step toward living the reality you desire.

- **If you skip this exercise**, you won't have a good picture of how you're using your time. If you feel like you have loads of time and starting a business will be a piece of cake, that's probably okay! You are the exception. But skipping this exercise will significantly stymie your progress if you are part of the other 99 percent.

Over the next seven days, take a few minutes at the end of each day to answer these two questions:

- What did I accomplish today? (List one or two items.)
- What did I *not* accomplish today? (List one or two items.)

Write down what comes to mind. The goal is not to write down the *hardest* or *most important* things you did on that day. Nor is it to write down what you *finished*: Progress toward a bigger goal is a worthy accomplishment!

At the end of the week, look back at your list and categorize each item using the eight categories listed above. Review your week. Which categories did you spend the most time on? Which categories fell right off your plate? After reviewing your week, set intentions for how you will spend your time for the next seven days. If important items like Sacred Space, Partnership, or Business Design received zero attention last week, be sure to commit to those areas for the next seven days.

EXERCISE 2: DOWN WITH DEVICE DISTRACTION

🕓 **Suggested Time to Complete:** Five to ten minutes.

✓ **When you complete this exercise,** your smartphone will be a whole lot smarter! You'll be cutting back on the dings, beeps, boops, and buzzes that draw you into Distracted Disservice.

⊗ **If you skip this exercise,** you'll be more susceptible to the endless scrolling and auto-play videos that put money in the pockets of social media ad gurus but rob you of time and energy.

A recent research study by SolitaireD, a gaming company, "revealed that 78 percent of respondents underestimated how much time they actually spent on their phones. The average estimate of phone use was three hours forty-two minutes, but the average actual daily usage time is five hours forty-two minutes."[28]

While the world throws many opportunities for distraction at us, these tiny supercomputers we keep tucked into our pockets can be a big one. Luckily, they also have built-in tools to monitor how we spend our device time. With these tools, you can monitor how much time you're spending on your device and what apps you're using. The tools on each phone may vary. You can find the information about your phone on our resources page at ApplePieMoms.com, or by scanning the QR code.

Take ten minutes now to review how you're using your device on a daily basis. Then take these three steps to cut down on your digital distractions:

1. Set daily time limits for the apps you're most likely to use as distractions.

2. Create a home screen widget for your tracking tool so that this information is there every time you pick up your phone.
3. Create friction! Move your most distracting apps to the last screen or remove them from your home screen altogether so that they are harder to access.

EXERCISE 3: TWO-WEEK, IN-DEPTH TIME AUDIT

You may consider revisiting this exercise after you have already begun planning your business or after it is launched. This exercise requires a two-week commitment and, understandably, you may want to wait until you can get the most benefit from your efforts.

In this exercise, you will track your time using the MAPHH Framework mentioned above. If you are ready for a serious evaluation of how you spend your time, then visit ApplePieMoms.com or scan the QR code to access our time-auditing tool and detailed instructions.

TIME BLOCKING

NOW THAT YOU UNDERSTAND HOW you spend your time, you can rework your days to design the integrated life of your dreams. But just knowing you want to spend more time with Sacred Space and less time on Family Management won't make it happen. The tool for making it happen is time blocking. This strategy was by far the most recommended strategy among the moms I interviewed for this book. It's a technique that I teach my team members to help them manage both their work and personal time. The strategy is simple. Basically, you add your tasks to your calendar and work your day according to your calendar. Here is a picture of mine.

My Life Theme:					
	Monday	Tuesday	Wednesday	Thursday	Friday
Personal Growth	X I've reviewed my Life Plan	I've reviewed my Life Plan	I've reviewed my Life Plan	I've reviewed my Life Plan	I've reviewed my Life Plan
	X I've reviewed my Goals	I've reviewed my Goals	I've reviewed my Goals	I've reviewed my Goals	I've reviewed my Goals
Project 1:					
	H: M: Reward	H: M: Reward	H: M: Reward	H: M: Reward	H: M: Reward
Project 2:					
	H: M: Reward	H: M: Reward	H: M: Reward	H: M: Reward	H: M: Reward
Project 3:					
	H: M: Reward	H: M: Reward	H: M: Reward	H: M: Reward	H: M: Reward
Appointments					
Client Work					
Marketing					
If this were the second time I lived this day, what would I do differently?					
Things I get to enjoy					

Each Sunday evening, I plan out my calendar a week at a time. I block off time for the big items, like writing this book every day. I block off meeting time with my team members to ensure that we're working together on important projects. I put all glass balls on the calendar and give them an appropriate time allotment. Then I have rubber balls to attend to each day, but not necessarily put into a time slot. My objective is to accomplish them that day, but if I don't, they are rubber and can bounce to the next day. For example, I always plan to write my blog post for the week on Tuesday. My hard deadline is Thursday. I know it makes my assistant's life harder if I wait until Thursday, though, so I give myself Tuesday to fit it in. If I haven't completed the blog by Tuesday night, it goes into my calendar for a specific time on Wednesday.

Time blocking gives me structure without being rigid. It will allow you to be as rigid or as loose as you want. I have been following this approach and tweaking it for many years. Setting my weekly plan, telling my accountability group what I will accomplish, committing to it with them, and then working through my plan, has been my secret weapon for living life on my terms and getting the important things done without dropping glass balls. Think about your "planning style" and what resonates with you.

The hardest part of trying something new when there are so many demands on your time is breaking out of your typical routine and operating differently than others might expect. It's not lost on me that, in this chapter on time management, I'm adding one more thing to your list when your days are already super busy and overscheduled. I also know that if you don't make a change and put some new time management techniques in place, you won't have the bandwidth to do the exercises in this book. Giving yourself the time to complete the exercises and get clear on your plans is required for you to move toward your dreams with confidence.

As you face doubts and criticism from your friends, family, and even yourself for moving in a new direction, you want to know that you've arrived at your decisions based on doing your homework. While it is important that you make time to do the work, often, that isn't enough. You need a little help from others who are also committed to the vision of creating an integrated family and business life. I've found that accountability partners provide the help needed to stay the course.

> PROGRESS NUGGET: *"I think every working mom probably feels the same thing: You go through big chunks of time where you're just thinking, 'This is impossible—oh, this is impossible.' And then you just keep going and keep going, and you sort of do the impossible."—Tina Fey*[29]

ACCOUNTABILITY PARTNERS

ANY TIME WE ARE TRYING to create a new "normal" for ourselves, having the dream and the data is not enough; we find ourselves right back in overwhelm and uneasiness. I, too, have felt totally at odds with who I am, my purpose, and how I should spend my time every day. The available time management tools seemed out of reach or just too much work to add to my already busy day. The approach that has helped me the most is using the tools consistently and monitoring my progress with the added component of "public" accountability. I participate in an accountability group of accountants that meets every Monday at 8:30 a.m. and has for many years. We spell out our quarterly goals for our businesses, our relationships, and our health. Every week, we each set the three action items for the upcoming week that will move us in the direction of our goals and report our progress on last week's action items.

There are many reasons these groups work. First, when you commit to your goals or plans in the presence of others, you are more likely to take action because you made that commitment. Second, your group will start to see your patterns and can call them to your attention. They can ask a question at the right time, such as, "This action has been incomplete for three weeks, why are you putting it off?" Often, we simply don't see our own issues. But when you have a trusted group that wants to see you succeed, they hold your feet to fire so you face your own BS.

An accountability group is a great way to maintain your focus and ensure that you are moving toward your goals. If you don't have a network to support you and hold you accountable, we have you covered. Go to ApplePieMoms.com or scan the QR Code below to join an accountability group facilitated by our partner, Acorn Mom. Taking these first steps is vital to your ultimate success, and they can help you immediately.

You picked up this book because you're yearning to create a life that has more balance and fulfillment than what's available to you in a traditional career, where a large part of your time is purchased from you and used in service of another's goals. While your desires are the spark that ignites the fire, examining and refining how you spend your time is the fuel that keeps it burning and growing.

By using the Motherhood, Apple Pie, and Happy Horseshit Framework and other tools in this chapter, you will create an overall life strategy. It requires big-picture visioning, strategic and operational planning, and tactical execution with a side of accountability. To some, this may seem over the top. I understand that we all have varying degrees of appreciation for planning. Some folks thrive on it and create plans and execute them with military precision. Others want to stay all "loosey-goosey" and strive not to be "pinned down." I fall somewhere in between. I feel adrift without a plan for the week and, while I may be busy, I don't feel productive. I don't like to be scheduled every minute of every day, though. I prefer to have a few firm commitments and a general plan for how I will work through my days.

The tools we offer provide flexibility in when and how you use them. If you didn't do the exercises in this chapter, go back and pick one that is the right fit for your needs. You don't have to do everything to start, but you do have to start if you want to integrate your entrepreneurial life and your personal life and live by design.

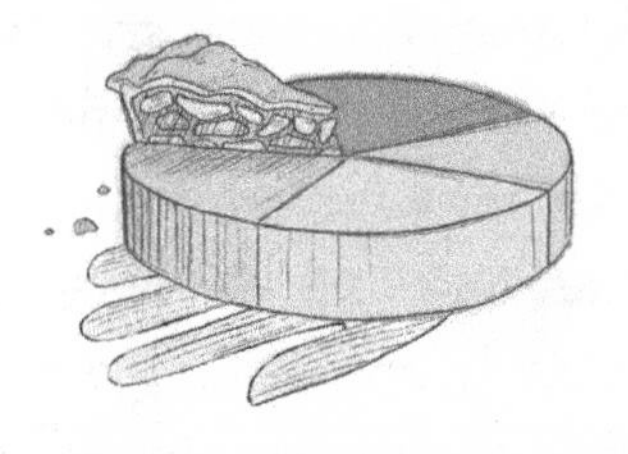

CHAPTER 7

CONNECT THE MONEY DOTS TO SECURE YOUR DREAMS

YOU'VE COME A LONG WAY in creating a life you want; one that is driven by your desires and your personal values. You've carved out and committed to a Sacred Space to think, solve problems, and dream. Within that Sacred Space, you've found answers to important questions about your priorities, your Immutable Laws, and how you want your child to perceive you and your work. You've started to build a support system to help you take action on your dreams and considered how to make time for this life you're designing. Now, it's time to fund it.

When your money works, it's easier to make your life and business work. Too often, big plans fall apart due to financial issues. When you think about your next move, to start a business or grow your business, connect the money dots so you can make it happen. The stakes are too important, and you are too emotionally invested to leave this to chance.

In July of 2015, when Alaina was sixteen, she decided to go to Brazil for a year as a Rotary exchange student. We said goodbye and I cried all the way home from the airport. She had been my life; and like a little bird, she flew away as children are supposed to do. Suddenly, my flexible job could absorb all my time. My husband had a new consulting job and was traveling Monday through Friday.

During weekdays, I took care of the animals, myself, and the property. I also worked from 9:00 a.m. until 6:00 p.m. and then was back at it from 7:00 p.m. until 10:00 p.m. My business was my refuge. I went from this intensely devoted mom life to being by myself with nothing to do but focus on my company.

For six months, from July until December of 2015, I lived two extremes. I worked like crazy as the business grew—and I was so incredibly lonely. Just before Christmas, the company my husband consulted for was sold and he was given the opportunity to move to their location in Indiana. We absolutely love our home and living on the creek, so he declined the offer and came home. I was so relieved and happy to have Dave home. But, it was a weird feeling because our primary source of income had just evaporated.

I asked Dave to consider waiting a couple of months to look for a new job and to help me with the year-end processes for our clients. In the bookkeeping world, the month of January is our busy season. Most clients have a fiscal year that ends in December and they need their yearly financial statements as soon as possible in order to get their taxes prepared. He pitched in and was so helpful.

In addition to January being a busy production month, it is also our highest sales month. Everyone either wants to get the prior year cleaned up or get started off right for the new year. The combination of new clients and extra year-end production meant there was plenty of work that needed Dave's attention. By mid-March, we had considered the growth projections for the business, along with our ability to make ends meet on less money, and decided that we could make it work financially to bring him into the business.

By the time Alaina returned in June, we both had offices at home and were working with our team remotely. Just as she had grown and changed, we had, too. She came back ready to start college, so we had to be serious about planning the family finances. This was the juncture in my life when my business grew up, too. It had to support all three of us, and there was no corporate job to fall back on.

Luckily for me, my business operated using Profit First. We paid ourselves first, set aside money for profit and taxes, and ran the business on everything else. We occasionally had to hit our savings account; it wasn't all roses. But we could quickly see when and where we went off-track and would right the train and move forward again.

My role with my clients grew from bookkeeping to advising on business profitability. We developed tools to help clients implement Profit First, understand profitability at the product level, and move from corporate day jobs with ecommerce side hustles to ecommerce businesses as their primary source of income.

Together, Dave and I connected the money dots so we could successfully keep him at home, live, and put our daughter through college without his consulting income. We found a way to create a life that made us both feel fulfilled. And if the money hadn't lined up, that dream would not have come to fruition.

We've helped our clients do the same using Profit First principles. You met Julia in an earlier chapter. Back in 2015, her husband, Jeremy, was working as a business analyst with a local bank near their home in Washington. Julia was at home managing their new ecommerce business and taking care of Wilder and JoJo. Jeremy helped out, too. His role in the business was managing inventory and accounting. Julia was more involved in brand development and product development and design.

Jeremy had a dream driven by his own personal values, and he needed to connect his family's money dots to make it happen. He said, "I want to develop a path so I can leave my job at the bank and work full-time in the business."

I asked him why he wanted to make that change and he was very clear. "I don't want my kids to only see me at dinner and bedtime," Jeremy replied. "I want to walk my kids to school in the morning and be there to walk them home in the afternoon."

Jeremy and Julia wanted real data before they took that important step of him leaving the bank, so we got busy and made a plan for him. We used the Owner's Pay calculator, which you'll learn about later in this chapter, to reverse engineer how much the business would have to make in sales to ensure he could pay himself a wage comparable to his "day job" pay. In 2017, Jeremy did leave his day job, and when JoJo started first grade, he walked her to school... and then walked back to his home office!

Up to this point in the book, we have focused on designing your life. In this chapter, let's take that design and bring it into tighter focus by developing a financial framework for both your family and business goals. You may have anxiety as you start this process because it is about money, and for a million and one reasons, money can be scary. Stay with me. We're going to break it down. Remember, this is what I do for my day job, and it's my goal to get you through this chapter so you know your next steps to set up your finances in a way that will work for you. The framework you create will show you the adjustments you need to make. Ultimately, it will give you confidence that you will be able to afford your lifestyle and invest in starting a business.

If you find that you can't make yourself do this work, we're here to help you. We have created a program that will provide the tools, training, and team to ensure that you have a financial plan that gives you confidence. Check out our website acornmom.com/apple-pie/exercise-help for the details.

PERSONAL FINANCES: STEPS 1 AND 2

As you've seen before in other chapters, I like to take stock of the situation before I initiate a project. We're going to do the same and start with taking stock of your personal finances. We begin with your personal situation so we know the amount of money your business will need to contribute to your life to keep you in a comfortable financial position.

Don't worry. You won't have to create a complicated budget. You need just a few key numbers to help understand the big picture and where to dive in deeper. You may know these numbers off the top of your head, or you might want to look at the last two to three months of bank statements to find them.

Let's start with some simple questions:

1. How much income do you currently have coming in each month? Is it steady or does it vary?
2. How much do you spend or need to spend each month to be comfortable?
3. How much money do you have in savings? Were you planning to use any of this to launch your business?
4. How much personal debt do you have? How much is it costing you each month in payments?

Follow along with the example below as we use my Personal and Business Financial Business Workbook to illustrate Taylor's financial journey. I will walk you through the exercises and what to think about in the right order. At the end of the example, you can download a copy of our blank workbook and complete this exercise for yourself. If this is at all intimidating to you, then read this chapter all the way through to understand the process and the result. Then come back and read each section again as you complete the exercises.

For Step 1, we will gather the personal information needed to understand the family income and expenses in a typical month. Taylor's family has an income of $3,000 per month with both parents working. Taylor works part-time and accounts for $500 of this monthly income. The family's expenses are $2,500 a month, which allows them to put $500 in savings each month. Overall, they have done a good job keeping debt down and have built up a nice savings of $10,000.

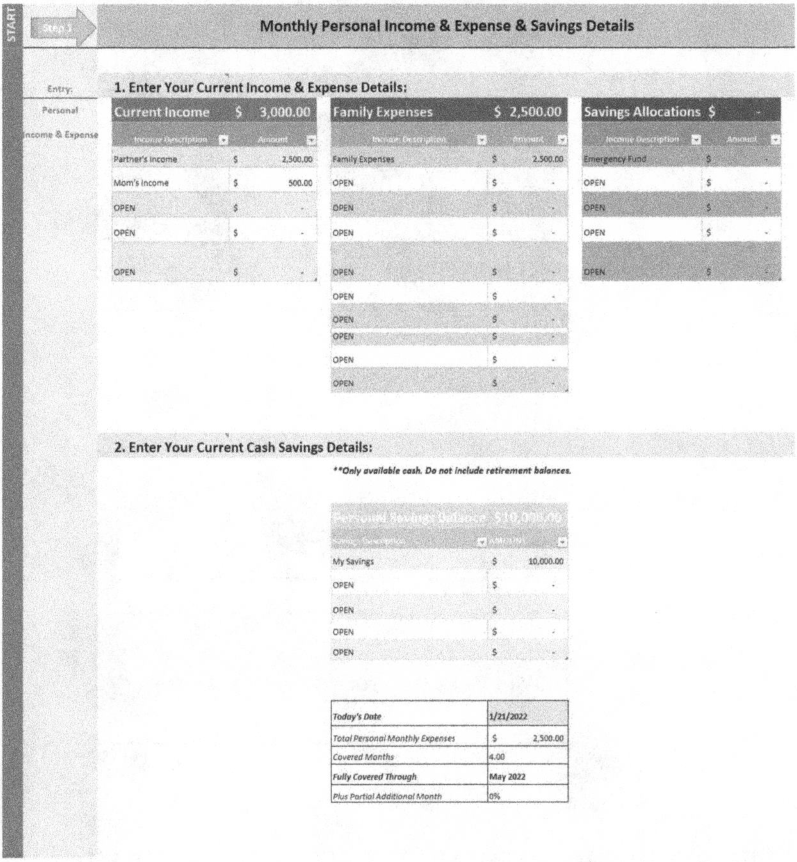

START

Step 1 → **Monthly Personal Income & Expense & Savings Details**

Entry:
Personal
Income & Expense

1. Enter Your Current Income & Expense Details:

Current Income	$ 3,000.00
Income Description	Amount
Partner's Income	$ 2,500.00
Mom's Income	$ 500.00
OPEN	$ -
OPEN	$ -
OPEN	$ -

Family Expenses	$ 2,500.00
Income Description	Amount
Family Expenses	$ 2,500.00
OPEN	$ -
OPEN	$ -
OPEN	$ -
OPEN	$ -
OPEN	$ -
OPEN	$ -
OPEN	$ -
OPEN	$ -
OPEN	$ -

Savings Allocations	$ -
Income Description	Amount
Emergency Fund	$ -
OPEN	$ -
OPEN	$ -
OPEN	$ -
OPEN	$ -

2. Enter Your Current Cash Savings Details:

***Only available cash. Do not include retirement balances.*

Personal Savings Balance	$10,000.00
[illegible]	Amount
My Savings	$ 10,000.00
OPEN	$ -
OPEN	$ -
OPEN	$ -
OPEN	$ -

Today's Date	1/21/2022
Total Personal Monthly Expenses	$ 2,500.00
Covered Months	4.00
Fully Covered Through	May 2022
Plus Partial Additional Month	0%

Step 2 is a review of this information, including the number of months your savings will cover your expenses should all income be lost. This is not an expected outcome, but a way to understand the risk to the family which could occur in a worst-case scenario. In their present situation, Taylor's family has four months' worth of expense coverage in their savings account.

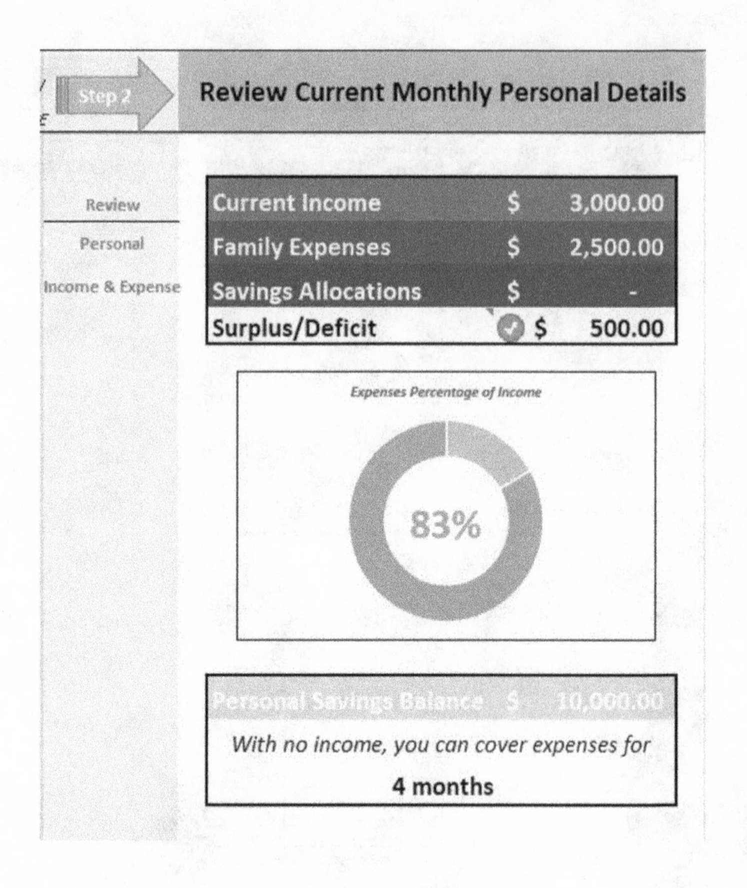

BUSINESS PLANNING WITH PROFIT FIRST: STEPS 3 AND 4

Taylor knows that she could eventually earn more money by starting her own business. She wants to leave her job and invest $5,000 of the family savings to start her business. This is half their savings and leaves the family with only two months' worth of expenses saved in case of an emergency. Also, like all businesses, Taylor's business will not necessarily generate income from day one.

Step 3: In this step, we will evaluate the impact of starting the business. This scenario is modeled in the chart below.

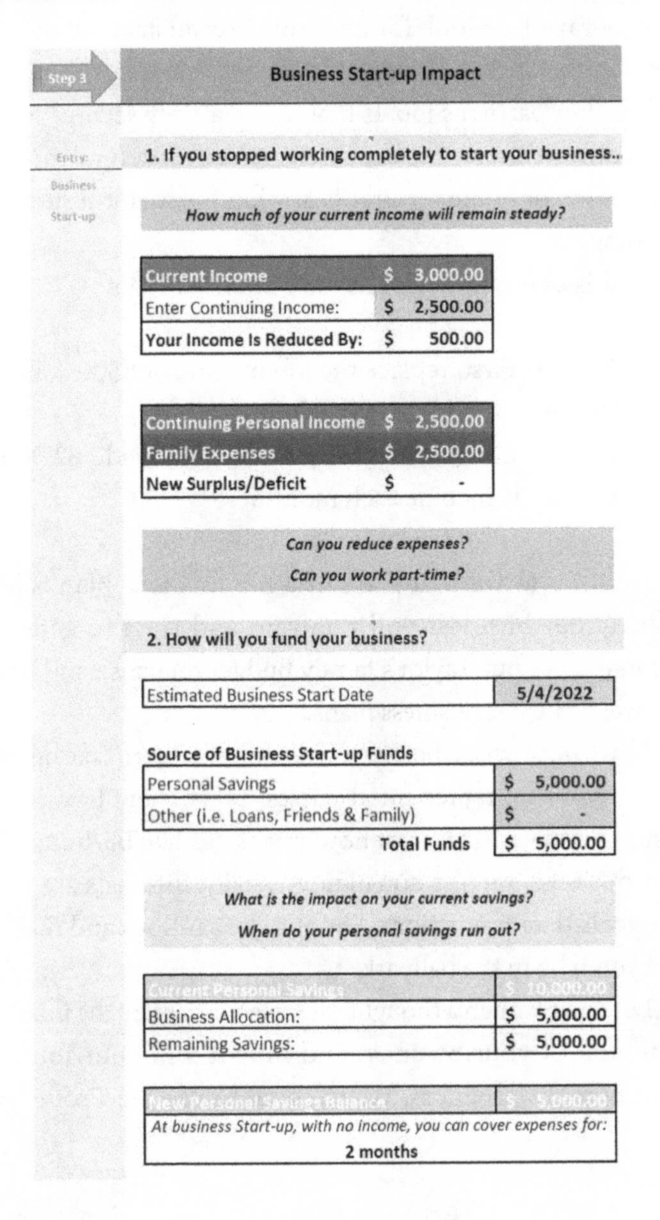

Step 3

Business Start-up Impact

Entry: Business Start-up

1. If you stopped working completely to start your business...

How much of your current income will remain steady?

Current Income	$ 3,000.00
Enter Continuing Income:	$ 2,500.00
Your Income Is Reduced By:	**$ 500.00**

Continuing Personal Income	$ 2,500.00
Family Expenses	$ 2,500.00
New Surplus/Deficit	**$ -**

Can you reduce expenses?

Can you work part-time?

2. How will you fund your business?

Estimated Business Start Date	5/4/2022

Source of Business Start-up Funds

Personal Savings	$ 5,000.00
Other (i.e. Loans, Friends & Family)	$ -
Total Funds	**$ 5,000.00**

What is the impact on your current savings?

When do your personal savings run out?

Current Personal Savings	$ 10,000.00
Business Allocation:	$ 5,000.00
Remaining Savings:	$ 5,000.00

New Personal Savings Balance	$ 5,000.00
At business Start-up, with no income, you can cover expenses for: **2 months**	

Based on this information, what should Taylor do? Should she go ahead and start her business, wait until she has more money saved, or look for investors? As an accountant, I'm programmed to say, "It depends." In our example, the income is from her partner's job. Is that job relatively secure? Might the family incur any big expenses in the next several months, such as car or home repairs? Is any kind of medical situation pending?

In this example, Taylor has two financial goals.

- **Goal 1**: First, replace the job income of $500 a month to continue adding to the family savings.
- **Goal 2**: Long-term. One year from now, add $2,000 to the family income each month.

Another factor that plays into her financial plan is how quickly her business will ramp up and start to generate income. Let's put Taylor's family budget on pause and begin to investigate her business plans.

I have one request before you read any further: Take off your rose-colored entrepreneurial glasses. Every client I work with is super excited to forecast how great sales will be, but with a new business, we just don't know. Really, forecasts are more like goals than predictions. Shoot to be cautious and realistic and you'll be in the ballpark.

Let's go through a thought exercise to evaluate the financial potential of your business and how it will contribute to your personal finances. We're going to use the Profit First framework created by Mike Michalowicz here. Once you decide to start your business, make sure you read his book, *Profit First*,[30] or one of the derivatives written for a specific industry. (See the list at ApplePieMoms.com scanning the QR code.)

For now, I'll guide you through how to think about your business in a way that will generate profits from day one and set you up to be successful. We'll keep this high-level exercise as simple as possible.

We'll use the example of a products-based business just to get the concept down, because the numbers are firm. Even if you are a service-based business, follow along to understand the concepts; they will translate easily. An example of a service-based business is included in the resources page at ApplePieMoms.com.

Step 4 estimates how much you will charge for your product and how many you expect to sell each month.

To begin, we need to start with sales and cost projections. Here is a short description of each of the major accounting terms used in the example.

Taylor is considering selling dog beds. Based on her research, she can sell them at forty dollars each. In discussions with a local manufacturer, she learned that her costs will be ten dollars per bed plus additional costs for packaging. The total cost of goods sold will be fifteen dollars.

Sales	Costs	Operating Expenses
Sales price per unit: This is what your customer will pay you for one unit or product. Market research is the best source to understand pricing for your product.	Cost of goods sold (COGS): This is the cost of the product that you pay to your supplier. If you are manufacturing, it's the cost of each item used to make your product along with the cost of the labor to assemble it. It also includes packaging.	Include items such as insurance, software to run your business, administrative labor, etc.
Unit sales per month: This is the number of sales you expect of the products during a typical month.	Cost of sales (COS): This is the cost of shipping and commissions for outside salespeople.	

Next, we need to estimate the cost of sales Taylor will incur to get her product in front of customers. She plans to sell online and learned from her entrepreneur group that 30 percent is a typical cost for commission, storage fees, and other expenses billed by the platform. Next, based on competitor data, Taylor has determined that she can sell 150 beds each month.

Finally, Taylor estimates her operating expenses. These are her expenses that aren't related to the production of dog beds. Marketing and advertising, insurance, software, and other administrative support services are a few examples.

Business Sales Projections

1 Estimate 1 unit sales price, cost of making, and cost of selling.

Sales Price Per Unit	$40.00
Cost of Goods (COGS) Per Unit	$15.00
Cost of Sale (COS) Per Unit	$12.00

2 Estimate how many you can sell each month.

Monthly Units Sold	150

**Seasonal Sales Note: Many businesses experience seasonality. If you'd like to account for seasonality in this workbook, divide your estimate across 12 months and add the monthly amount to step 2 entry.*

3 Estimate your monthly Operating Expenses (OpEx).

Monthly OpEx*	$500.00

**Do not include: Owner Pay or Personal Salary. This will be calculated during the Profit First allocation.*

Revenue Review	Monthly	Annual
Estimated Units Sold:	150	1800
Esimated Selling Price Per Unit:	$40.00	
Estimated Revenue	$ 6,000.00	$ 72,000.00

COGS Review	Monthly	Annual
Estimated Total COGS per month	$ 2,250.00	$ 27,000.00

COS Review	Monthly	Annual
Estimated Total COS per month	$ 1,800.00	$ 21,600.00

Gross Profit	$ 1,950.00	$ 23,400.00
Gross Margin	33%	33%

Operating Expenses (OpEx), Payroll, and Net Profit are paid from Gross Profit.
Gross Margin is so important because you need enough cash flowing down the funnel.

OpEx Review	Monthly	Annual
Estimated Total OpEx per month	$500.00	$ 6,000.00

The spreadsheet provides a simple review of your data so you can evaluate whether your product meets the minimum suggested profitability goals. We have done all the number-crunching—what does it tell us? Now we'll move from number-crunching to interpreting the data.

This is your first place to check your results. What you want to learn from your data at this level is: Does your product generate enough money at the gross profit margin (GPM) level to justify proceeding? A general rule of thumb in business is that you must make a gross profit margin of more than 30 percent. This number is important because if you don't generate a gross profit margin of 30 percent, you will not have enough money to pay yourself, taxes, or operating expenses. When I see businesses operate below 30 percent GPM, they must typically borrow money to survive and that starts them in a downward spiral. When you borrow money, the interest expense must be repaid. When your GPM is already stretched, you simply don't have enough money to cover another cost, such as interest.

This is the point to stop and truly dive into your pricing and costs. Don't gloss over this step; it is the key to building a successful business. Investigate: Are there other pricing models that will allow you to charge more, or other suppliers that can produce your product at a lower cost? This is where you can get creative and innovative.

Yes, this step is ultimately a numbers game, but it is also a marketing step. It's about understanding what your customers value and how to develop your product in a way that pricing is not their primary concern. Also, consider the unique value that you can bring to your customers. When you understand how to meet your customers' needs in a way that no one else can, it makes it easier to price your product or service above the market rate. Recognize your worth and don't undervalue yourself. As you solve these marketing questions, your numbers game will get easier simply because you have more cash available to fund your lifestyle and future business growth.

If your GPM didn't meet the 30 percent target, stop here with these exercises. Get this issue solved before continuing with the exercises or your business launch. Double-check, here: Are you wearing rose-colored glasses? If so, take them off, review these numbers again, and get real with yourself.

PROFIT FIRST MAGIC: STEP 5

Let's get serious about Profit First. Profit First is a money system that allows you to always know your cash position simply by looking at your bank accounts. It helped me understand that paying myself first and setting aside money for taxes ensured that I operated with efficiency, frugality, and innovation. As I coach my clients on this simple system, I see how they start to understand their finances—often for the first time. It really does work like magic to secure your business dreams. Please make a vow to me right now that you will not skip over this section. It is the secret sauce that will make you profitable from day one, and it will put the right pressures on your business to ensure that it takes care of you, your family, and your obligation as a taxpayer. People who ignore this process often end up hating their business because it always takes money from them and never gives back. It also puts you in the difficult position of justifying yourself to your family. You will already be dividing your time; you don't want to add money problems to this equation.

In Step 5, we see that Taylor's sales deposits into her bank account total $4,200. This is the total monthly revenue of $6,000 generated from sales less the cost of sales ($1,800). In this case, the cost of sales was deducted by the platform before they made her sales deposit to her bank account. Now, consider how much of that money Taylor will need to replace the product sold. We have that information based on our earlier work. Our COGS is fifteen dollars per unit, and we know Taylor sold 150 units. $2,250 will be needed to replace this product when she orders again.

Set the $2,250 aside to replenish inventory so you won't touch it. Create a separate bank account designated for inventory. Make it a rule and a habit: As you collect money for items sold, always move the funds to replace those items in your Inventory account. A magic moment will occur when you make your next inventory buy: You will have the money needed for the purchase and will not be scrambling to find the cash.

If Taylor sees rapid growth in her sales, she should set aside an additional percentage above the replenishment costs to pay for larger inventory orders in the future. If you have to deplete your personal funds or borrow money, you are putting a lot of pressure on yourself and your business. Most businesses, especially start-ups, do not have a large enough margin to cover expensive debt.

The rest of the Profit First magic is allocating the remaining $1,950 to bank accounts for specific purposes. Think of it like the envelope system, but for your business. You stash away a percentage of your Real Revenue to cover necessary business expenses, like paying your team and saving for essential equipment, various taxes, and of course—profit. As I recommended earlier, read *Profit First* and the derivatives that relate to your industry to learn more about the appropriate allocations for businesses in your industry. I'm going to give you an example based on the percentages shared in the original book.

	A	B	C	D	E	F
Real Revenue Range	$0 - $250k	$250k - $500k	$500k - $1m	$1m - $5m	$5m - $10m	$10m - $50m
Real Revenue	100%	100%	100%	100%	100%	100%
Profit	5%	10%	15%	10%	15%	20%
Owner's Pay	50%	35%	20%	10%	5%	0%
Tax	15%	15%	15%	15%	15%	15%
Operating Expenses	30%	40%	50%	65%	65%	65%

In addition to the Inventory checking account that we've discussed, you will want five more bank accounts for the following purposes: Income, Profit, Owner's Pay, Tax, and Operating Expenses (OpEx). As long as interest rates are low, it's fine to set them all up as checking accounts.

Your money will flow like this:

From the first to the fifteenth of each month, all deposits will go into your Income account.

On the fifteenth, take those funds deposited and allocate the Cost of Goods sold amount to your Inventory bank account. The amount that remains is known as Real Revenue. The remaining allocations are applied to the Real Revenue.

Continuing with Taylor's example and using $1,950 as Real Revenue (even though we're doing this for half the month, we'll stick with these numbers to make this easier to follow), multiply $1,950 x the percentages for each bank account as follows:

$1,950 Real Revenue x 5% = $97.50 for Profit. *YAY!! The business made a profit!*

$1,950 Real Revenue x 50% = $975 for Owner's Pay. *YAY!! Your first paycheck!*

$1,950 real revenue x 15% = $292.50 for Taxes. *YAY!! The IRS is covered next April!*

$1,950 real revenue x 30% = $585 for Operating Expenses. *Hmm, I gotta be frugal!*

Below is a table to show you the process all the way through.

Step 5

Profit First

This is where it all comes together.

The business runs on the sales deposits in the bank.

Profit First:

Allocate

Cash Deposits

Review

1 Sales Deposits*		Monthly	Annual
Estimated Cash into the Bank		$ 4,200.00	$ 50,400.00

*Revenue minus Cost of Sales

2 Profit First Categories		Monthly	Annual
Inventory		$ 2,250.00	$ 27,000.00
Real Revenue Available		$ 1,950.00	$ 23,400.00
Profit	5%	$ 97.50	$ 1,170.00
Owner Pay	50%	$ 975.00	$ 11,700.00
Income Taxes	15%	$ 292.50	$ 3,510.00
Operating Expenses	30%	$ 585.00	$ 7,020.00

3 OpEx Allocation	Monthly	Annual
OpEx Cash Available	$ 585.00	$ 7,020.00
Enter Your Business OpEx:	$ 500.00	$ 6,000.00
OpEx Surplus/Deficit	$ 85.00	$ 1,020.00

Is there enough allocated cash to cover OpEx?

4 Personal Income & Expenses	Monthly	Annual
Stable Monthly Income:	$ 2,500.00	$ 30,000.00
Plus Owner Pay:	$ 975.00	$ 11,700.00
Plus Profit Distribution:	$ 97.50	$ 1,170.00
Total Income Update	$ 3,572.50	$ 42,870.00
Total Monthly Expenses	$ 2,500.00	$ 30,000.00
Personal Surplus/Deficit	$ 1,072.50	$ 12,870.00

On a 12-month basis, your personal surplus/deficit is:
$ 12,870.00

Can you increase sales prices?
Can you increase the number of units sold?
Can you decrease product costs?
Can you decrease fulfillment costs?

Now you can see that a healthy business sets aside money for replenishing inventory, makes a profit, pays the owner, and takes care of the obligation to the government. The remaining dollars are used to operate the business. As I mentioned before, this keeps the pressure on to remain lean, efficient, frugal, and innovative. It is tempting to say, "I won't pay myself because I have another source of income." I still encourage you to set that money aside in an Owner's Pay account. If something changes and you need income, or if you can't work and have to hire someone, you need to be prepared to cover the salary of the most important employee in the business—you.

The Profit account has two functions. First of all, it rewards you for being a business owner. Every quarter, you will pay yourself half of the funds from the Profit account and do something for yourself and your family as a reward for the risk and effort you have put in as a business owner. I don't recommend reinvesting the money in the business because the business becomes dependent on those funds to operate. The other half of the funds will stay in the Profit account to begin building your business emergency fund. The goal is to build up a reserve that will cover your business expenses should your income sources be delayed or you have unusual expenses to pay. The health of your Profit account becomes a measure of health for your business.

THE WHOLE KIT AND CABOODLE

WE HAVE LOOKED AT YOUR personal financial needs, and we've looked at your business and know it will generate cash, so now let's put them together. A quick overview of Taylor's personal income and expenses are shown in #4 of the Step 5

Profit First chart above. She can pay herself $975 each month, which exceeds her income from her previous job. In addition, she will be able to take profit distributions every quarter.

Another approach is to use our Owner's Pay calculator to help you reverse engineer how the business will help you achieve your personal income goals.

Remember, in the personal example, Taylor's income from her job was $500 a month. She has two goals.

- **Goal 1**: First, replace the job income of $500 a month to continue to add to the family savings. Taylor has been successful in meeting this goal!
- **Goal 2**: Long-term. One year from now, add $2,000 to the family income each month. Let's look at how the business must perform to reach Goal 2.

How much must she sell to reach Goal 2 of $2,000 a month in income? Using the Owner's Pay calculator, we can plug in our numbers and get answers. We simply need to add three pieces of information that we have already generated. When we add this information, we learn the amount of business revenue needed to achieve this goal.

Let's do it! When you open the calculator online at ApplePieMoms.com or scan the QR Code, complete these three steps:

Step 1: Set the Real Revenue tier of your business. We determined this in the previous section, "Profit First Magic." Our example shows that real revenue will be $23,400, so we fall into Tier A in the chart. If you are unsure of your initial sales level, start with Tier A until you have data to support another starting point.

Step 2: Add your personal target annual income. Taylor needs $2,000 a month times twelve months, which is $24,000.

Step 3: Add your anticipated business gross margin. In our example, the gross margin was 33 percent.

You can see the completed calculations. Taylor needs to generate $12,121 in sales revenue each month.

MOTHERHOOD, APPLE PIE, and all that HAPPY HORSESHIT

Owner Pay Calculator

Enter only 3 pieces of data to generate your target revenue!

Step 1 - Identify Your Profit First Tier

Using the reference chart below, find the tier linked to your real revenue amount (A, B, C, D, E, F).

Reference For Profit First Tier Selection

Profit First Tier	A	B	C
Real Revenue Range	$0 - $250K	$250K - $500K	$500K - $1M
Real Revenue %	100%	100%	100%
Profit	5%	10%	15%
Owner's Pay	50%	35%	20%
Tax	15%	15%	15%
Operating Expenses	30%	40%	50%

Enter Your Tier: A

Step 2 - What's Your Desired Personal Income?

How much income do you need to support your family?

Enter Target Income: $2,000.00

Step 3 - What's Your Business Gross Margin?

Check your profit and loss (P&L) and divide your gross profit by top line revenue.
If you are unsure, start at a 30% target minimum.

Enter Business Gross Margin: 33%

Step 4 - Review Calculations Section & Results Section

Calculations

You entered the following:

Desired Personal Income	$2,000.00
Real Revenue Range	A
Gross Margin	33%

Here are the calculated numbers:

Top Line Revenue	$	12,121.21
COGS/Inventory	$	8,121.21
Real Revenue	$	4,000.00

Profit First Tier A	Percentages		Dollars
Real Revenue %	100%	$	4,000.00
Profit	5%	$	200.00
Owner's Pay	50%	$	2,000.00
Tax	15%	$	600.00
Operating Expenses	30%	$	1,200.00

Results

To earn $2,000.00, here's your real revenue:	$	4,000.00
With a gross margin of 33%, you must generate:	$	12,121.21

This is the place to do your reality check, another moment to remove those rose-colored glasses! Can you sell $145,000 worth of products in your first year? Will you be able to run your business with $14,400 in operating expenses to make this goal? Take a few moments or a few weeks, whatever is necessary, to truly work these numbers and see if the effort you put in will likely achieve your goals. It is human nature to fall in love with an idea to the point where you overlook its possible downsides. Brainstorm what the problems might be, then consider your solutions to those problems. Will you have to move mountains or simply tamp down a molehill?

Dave wanted to transition from consulting to working in my business so we could stay in Arkansas and have more time together. He was able to start helping me out right away, but ultimately, we had to grow to keep him at home and cover the loss of his consulting income. Jeremy wanted to spend more time with his kids, but he had to grow the business before he could quit his job. Being realistic is super important because your family's finances and your time with your family will be impacted. If these two factors, time and money, are out of kilter, then you have just added a tremendous amount of stress to your life. Remember, in our example, Taylor wanted to add to her monthly income to ensure her family could meet their typical monthly expenses. The worst outcome would be to spend savings and bring in no additional income. I don't mean to dampen anyone's dreams, but I have counseled many folks who jumped into the deep end of the pool when they didn't know how to swim. The flailing around represents real stress.

What if your numbers show that you don't have a viable business, at least at the start? First of all, bring it up with your accountability group on the Acorn Mom platform. They are business owners like you who can help give you some perspective and brainstorm solutions in a constructive, empathetic way. Then, armed with new ideas, dig in and begin to evaluate every part of your plan. Do you have the right business model? Could you structure your product offering differently, maybe add a subscription? How much can you sell at a higher price? What impact would that have on your gross margin? Is there a cheaper supplier or an alternative way to produce your product? Is there a local option that may be a little more expensive but cuts down your shipping costs more than enough to offset the increase, plus allows you to order at a lower minimum order quantity, freeing up your cash? If your market is too small, what about looking at related markets that could use your product without much modification?

In the end, if the numbers just don't work, take a deep breath and be grateful that you know now, while your only investment is in time and paper. Keep your thinking cap on, and over the coming weeks, you'll either come up with a better business idea or you'll see a way to make this one work. This is not the end.

My friend Kasey, a mom of two school-aged children and an accountant in the Boston area, loves restaurants. She dreamed of opening a coffee/bakery business. She had the concept in mind for years; she had a name, branding, and a menu ready to roll out when the right location came along. Kasey is a numbers gal, but she has a great flair for marketing, too. She knew that location would be key to the success of her business. She would see a property come onto the market from time to time in her local area, which would cause her dream to come to the forefront again. She would contact the realtor and visit the property, but it was never the right fit.

Finally, Kasey's dream location opened up. It had been a corner gas station for the previous fifty years, and she knew she could turn it into the perfect coffeehouse with a vintage theme. The property owners were ready to sell, yet ultimately the town would not approve the location for a coffeehouse. Kasey was bummed, but in her typical, resilient fashion, she brushed off her disappointment and put the idea back in its familiar location—the back of her mind. What came next surprised me. I think it also surprised her.

On the first day of a marketing retreat that Kasey and I attended, we discussed our projects. She shared that she was there to develop the marketing for a new book she is currently writing, *Profit First for Restaurants*. The coffee shop location didn't work, but her years-long exploration into starting the business and her prior experience as a restaurant owner helped Kasey understand how important it is to her to work with restaurants. Starting down a path that ultimately didn't work out helped her see her next steps. If your location doesn't work or your numbers don't "add up," that is just a step on your journey. Don't let it be the end of your journey.

> PROGRESS NUGGET: *Your vision will become clear only when you can look into your own heart. Who looks outside, dreams; who looks inside, awakes.*
> *—Carl Jung*[31]

STRIKING OUT ON YOUR OWN

ALICIA REACHED A POINT IN her career where she had to make a change. She is an accountant and worked remotely, starting

with her first child. After she had her third child, it didn't work anymore.

"Finally, I hit the point where I had to say, 'I can't handle this stress of feeling like I'm not making anyone happy, my coworkers or my family,'" Alicia told me. "I have three small kids. I can't be stressed all the time. There's year-end tax planning and they're on Christmas break from school, or they're on spring break and I have a corporate tax deadline and then individual taxes in April. With all these tax deadlines falling at the important times for my family, I looked at my life and realized I was going to live a miserable life, just wishing time away."

Many of us trying to juggle a corporate career and a family realize at some point that there has to be a better way. When Alicia reached that point, she took action. She explained, "I left the corporate world with just a couple clients, and I did some consulting work with them. As my youngest got a little bit older, I could see a way to add to my workload. I was very strategic in the amount of work that I picked up because I always wanted to be flexible. With my children's schedules, I didn't want to work an eight-to-five. I selected, very strategically, the types of work I would take on.

"Included in that selection process was knowing exactly what we need to live on. Between what my husband was making and what I was making, what amount of income met the bare minimum? Then anything additional was just gravy. We've both been very blessed with very flexible jobs. We're setting ourselves up so that we can have this flexible life and this time with our children without creating debt that would require payments that we can't afford. We're very cognizant of where we're spending our money. There's nothing wrong if people like new cars and all this kind of stuff, but we realize there's a tradeoff for it. For both of us, our goals are for our family time together, and having that open dialogue helps us maintain that as our priority. It sounds so cliché, but as a couple, we can dream together and have that common ground."

Like Wendy, Julia, and Jeremy, Alicia decided that the tradeoff for working in a traditional job was to have less time with her kids. Each of them decided to get smart about their personal finances and their business numbers. Understanding their numbers allowed them to move forward with a plan to prioritize their family.

Now it's time to work your numbers and connect your own money dots. You must consider your personal financial situation. You must consider the profitability of your business and determine if you will make a reasonable gross margin. You must calculate cash flow. And you must see how the business will pay you, and if your efforts will generate the Real Revenue to make it a healthy business and worth your investment of time. If you're not at this point in your decision-making yet, that's fine. This chapter will be right here when you are. Make a commitment now to come back to it because it is too important to skip!

PROFIT FIRST WORKBOOK

Suggested Time to Complete: This entire exercise will take you one to one-and-a-half hours. However, we advise breaking it into steps.

- Steps 1 and 2, Personal Income and Expense Review: thirty minutes or more. If you already keep a personal budget and expense record, this step should go fairly quickly. If you've never tracked this information, it will take longer.

- Step 3, Business Start-up Review: ten minutes.
- Step 4, Sales Projection: fifteen minutes.
- Step 5, Profit First Allocation Review: ten minutes.

⊘ **When you complete this exercise,** you will have a deep understanding of your business's financial health, including the estimated business profits needed to pay yourself and run the business.

⊗ **If you skip this exercise**, your business's ability to pay you and have the cash flow necessary to continue growing and thriving will be compromised. This exercise is completely necessary for keeping your business healthy.

⧗ ***Fast Five:*** You will need to complete this exercise in full, eventually. Take a minute now to block time to do the exercises. Additionally, schedule time with your partner or a trusted advisor (or both!) to talk about your goals and how they might impact your family financially and in other ways.

If you don't have a trusted advisor you are comfortable discussing these topics with, please email us at julia@acornmom.com or scan the QR code to reach out for assistance.

OWNER'S PAY CALCULATOR

Suggested Time to Complete: Five minutes.

When you complete this exercise, you will set a personal income goal and know how much revenue your business must generate to pay you that amount.

If you skip this exercise, you run the risk of either not paying yourself adequately (or at all) or overpaying yourself, leaving your business starved for cash and unable to grow.

Fast Five: Hey, now, this exercise only requires you to enter *three* numbers. Owning a business means you'll be paying yourself. Otherwise, you're just making a hobby of selling things. Let's figure this out!

If you're really unsure or haven't started your business yet, select Tier A in Step 1 and follow the other prompts in the workbook.

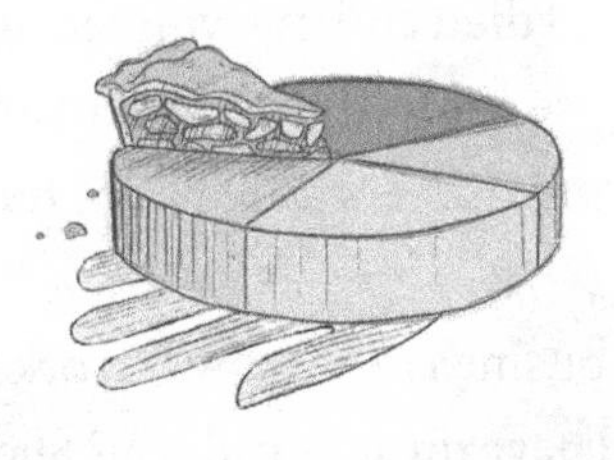

CHAPTER 8

BAKE MOTHERHOOD AND YOUR VALUES INTO THE BUSINESS CULTURE

WITH YOUR MINDSET IN THE right place and a better handle on how you will manage your time and finances, you are ready to develop your business from the aspect of possibility, not from how it's always been done.

As I've said before, your business is here to serve *you,* so build it that way. When I wanted remote work and flexibility, I found the QuickBooks online software and realized that cloud accounting would give me the chance to work at home or anywhere with an internet connection. With just that simple framework, I built my business. Then I added employees and services built around my values.

In the beginning, I was the only bookkeeper, and then I added an employee to help. I found her entirely by happenstance, but the story of how it happened makes a perfect point about how honoring your values will attract the right people to you. My washing machine had died and my wonderful repairman, John, was here at the house rebuilding it. He overheard my phone calls with clients and as he was leaving, he said, "Can I ask what you do?"

I explained my business and how it worked for me.

John said, "Can I have my wife call you? She is an accountant, and we have three girls in school. She would love to work from home instead of going into someone's office."

John's wife Amy called, and we had a great talk. We both valued flexibility and when that became clear, I began to see how I could grow a business beyond just me. At the end of our conversation, I offered her a job and she accepted.

A few years later, as I began to specialize in the ecommerce niche, I found ecommerce sellers who also valued lifestyle flexibility. Over time, we renegotiated with our legacy clients and handled our meetings via video conference. Through attrition, we lost clients who expected me to come to their office. I was fine with that; they needed something different than what I was willing to offer. Someone else would be a better fit for them. With this change, my business was in alignment with what I valued most: lifestyle flexibility. My clients and my employees are all comfortable on remote platforms and technology and it is easy to work together.

Growing a small business made me more aware of the importance of using our values as the underpinning of the culture we wanted for the business. There is a famous saying, often attributed to Peter Drucker, that "culture eats strategy for breakfast."[32] It is likely that many firms in your space will have vision, direction, and strategy in common. What will set you apart and appeal to the group of customers you are seeking because you are aligned with them is your values. When I first set my values for my business, I interviewed clients and asked them what made me unique in their eyes. They told me that they perceived a sense of calm as we talked and that they knew I cared about and could trust me. These comments were top-of-mind when I developed my initial values.

As we grew and focused more on culture, we looked for ways to ensure that these values were alive for each team member. This, along with our clearly defined Immutable Laws, helped us grow in a way that made sense for me, my family, and our team. (I find it helpful to think of Immutable Laws as the boundaries we do not cross and values as aspirational behaviors.) In this chapter, I'll share how to create your values, how to make them memorable, and how to keep them alive by using them to set the direction of your business and make day-to-day decisions.

SHARE VALUES WITH YOUR TEAM

Values are not a one-and-done exercise you do to check a box, or text for an inspirational poster to hang on your wall and forget about as if it was just part of your decor. Getting clarity and stating your values is an exercise to tap into your beliefs and determine how to turn those beliefs into behaviors.

Years ago, at my corporate job, our first exercise to move forward with our "Motherhood and Apple Pie" reorganization was to develop a list of words that represented our shared values. Through much discussion and deliberation, we came up with six words that encompassed our values. Our next step was to develop five sentences for each word to show what our behavior would be if we truly lived each value. The question we applied to each value statement was, "We'll know we are living the XXX value when we..."

Each person in the organization took time to develop these and, in an all-staff meeting, we shared the sentences that demonstrated a value particularly well. After we discussed the nuances of these statements, a small team reviewed the complete list of statements, pared them down, combined those that were similar, and refined them with an eye toward clarity. Then the entire organization had one more chance to discuss and refine before the leadership team adopted them as our values. The result was that each value had four to five statements to help us know when we were living those values. This document became our internal creed. Management made decisions and then reviewed them to ensure that they aligned with our values. We expected team members to question decisions if they thought they were outside of our values.

On occasion, we did act in ways that went against the values and didn't stop to consider them. That was always a tough conversation and realization, but the honesty between team members and the leadership group demonstrated the adherence to our values even though it was difficult. Reconsidering decisions and coming up with a result that was truly in alignment with our values always made us stronger as an organization. Not just because we had made a better decision, but because we had honored our team members, our values, and our process. It made it easier to deal with the next misstep because we all felt confident that we could get through it.

While living your business values is important, they must also be accessible to your team. When I initially developed the values for bookskeep, they were about what I wanted as a business owner. I didn't involve my small team at the time because their roles in the organization were part-time; and, in the end, it was my business. As my coach, Mike Michalowicz encouraged me to focus on the expectations I had for the business.

To be clear, my values didn't change once I got input from the team; we just viewed them through a more clearly defined lens. We built on the values I had set when I started bookskeep—lifestyle flexibility—and then focused on how we would serve our customers. I created a full list of values and worked with my team to define their meanings. Learning to live those values every day was another matter.

USE YOUR VALUES IN DAILY OPERATIONS

I KNEW WE HAD A problem because we had eight values, and I could only name four or five. They didn't trip off my tongue. If I couldn't remember them, how could I expect my team members to know them? And if we didn't know them, how could we live them and hold each other to the standards those values exemplified? I knew we had an issue, but it wasn't a glass ball issue. It was a nagging concern that I knew I would need to address someday.

I discovered my solution when I visited with Jesse Cole, owner of the Savannah Bananas baseball team. Jesse has reinvented baseball in Savannah and made it fun! I'm not a huge fan of baseball because it involves what seem like long stretches of inactivity; I'm much more drawn to basketball. However, Jesse has turned his baseball games and the entire experience of being a "banana fan" into a fan-first experience. Fun and entertainment are the objectives of the game!

When I toured the facilities and talked to Jesse before a game, I asked him about his values and the values of the Savannah Bananas. He shared with me that gratitude is an important personal value and, to practice gratitude, he recently spent a year writing at least one thank-you letter each night before he went to bed. The letters were to authors who have written books that inspired him, or to friends who shared meaningful insights, or to a grade school teacher from years ago. The responses to the letters also added richness to his life because he saw how his expressions of gratitude had a deep impact on the people who have impacted him. I was intrigued and I wanted to know more about his values.

Jesse quickly rattled them off. "Always be: caring, different, enthusiastic, fun, growing, and hungry."

In his book, *Find Your Yellow Tux*, Jesse discusses the creation of values and shares a secret that has helped me and my team immensely. Jesse had the same problem remembering his values, so he simply placed them in alphabetical order. Once he had a mnemonic, he could remember them.[33] What a simple and effective approach. I sat down with my list and asked myself, *What words represent my current list of values and would work in alphabetical order?* Some of them worked, like "data-driven" and "gratitude," but others we tweaked a bit; for example, "integrity" became "honesty." Here's what we ended up with:

Always **B**e: **C**aring, **D**ata-driven, **E**ducating, **F**lexible, **G**rateful, **H**onest, and **I**nquiring. Keeping the values easy to remember means they are accessible, at the ready for my team to use when a situation comes up. How could they influence our decisions when we couldn't remember them?

Our values are firm foundational blocks, but that doesn't mean that we set them and forget them. Values must be taught, understood, and tested. They should be a part of your organizational meetings, not just set dressing. When the leadership team acts in conflict with company values, the team members are responsible for holding up the mirror and asking if the action is in alignment with those values. While this is never fun, it is what keeps the values alive, dynamic, and relevant. You want to give them adequate consideration and ensure that they are meaningful to you. Then find ways to talk about them every time you're together.

At our meeting yesterday, we had a values scavenger hunt on Zoom. Not surprisingly, the team member who had them posted on the wall won! Caring is one of our values, and I was hearing from my team members that they were having trouble with time management. This was a perfect opportunity to exercise our value of educating and teach a class on goal-setting and time blocking. As a follow-up to the class, a few team members shared their specific time management challenges related to caring for preschool-aged children.

In the meeting wrap-up, these moms shared how helpful it was to hear that others were juggling and struggling. One said, "I thought it was just me that had to work late at night! I thought I was the only one not able to get it all done during the day." These ladies lacked a support community of women in the same situation. We held a meeting to talk more. That conversation led to a chat channel in our internal network focused on their issues. We also set up a quarterly meeting to address their specific problems, stay connected, and support each other.

Another time to use your values is when hiring your team. At bookskeep, we strive to deliver trust and peace of mind in every client communication. Our values of always being caring, data-driven, and honest are on display with every call and email. In fact, because we are never face to face with clients, it is even more important to get it right every time. To ensure that we hire team members who can achieve this standard, I ask potential employees two dealbreaker questions. At the conclusion of the interview, I ask, "If you were offered this job, what would it mean to you?" I want to know why they want the job. I developed this question because many of our best employees told me about their personal situations and concluded their stories with, "This job would be an answer to a prayer." When you answer someone's prayers, you can bet that they care and will care about their fellow team members and their clients.

The second question I ask is for them to rank the following six words in order of importance, with number one being most important: service, sales, quality, integrity, teamwork and profitability. After they share their rankings, I ask them to explain. If integrity is not number one, I get suspicious. If it's ranked a three or below, they are not considered further for the position. I will give them a chance to explain if they select it for the second position, and it better be good! I have only hired one person who made that selection, and they were using a lesser-known definition of the word that is not as common in our part of the country.

You see, when you truly live your values, you work to keep them alive; you don't put them away and consider them done. When you are building your business, it's your opportunity to make it work for you. You will find that your effort in this area will save you so much effort in making policy. The right things will get done in the right way because your team knows what is important.

YOUR VALUES CAN EVOLVE, JUST LIKE YOUR BUSINESS—AND YOU

YOUR VALUES CAN ALSO ADAPT over time. When I first developed mine, they omitted "inquiring." We decided it was important and needed to be included when we failed to provide excellent service to a client. I'll call him Peter.

I met Peter when he attended a talk I gave. He always added comments on my business and personal Facebook posts. He was a fan. He was a responsive client and always prompt in answering our questions and getting us what we needed. He worked hard to dial in and grow his business, and he took our message that it is vital to have confidence in your numbers to heart. He was a model client and considered us a partner.

We sent out Peter's monthly financials in June and he questioned them. His inventory and COGS number did not make sense to him. Dave took the lead and did a deep dive into the activity in those two accounts. He went over what was being paid for from these accounts with Peter. The answer was in plain sight: He had bought expensive photography equipment, not to resell as he did many items, but to use when photographing his products. It didn't belong in inventory, and removing it made his profitability plummet. It had been a year of rebuilding and pivoting for Peter, and he was seeing good profitability and not questioning the rest of his financials. But what he saw was a false result. He was frustrated with us for making an incorrect assumption that all equipment was inventory and frustrated that his pivot was not as successful as expected.

We owned the mistake because of our honesty value. We tried to make amends by providing extra services to Peter and we instituted extra oversight of his account to ensure that he didn't have issues in the future. He is still a client, and we work well together, but he had a lapse in confidence with us and I don't know if it will ever be completely restored.

Dave and I talked about what happened and how it happened. It was an easy mistake to understand, as Peter often bought items to resell on Amazon because that was his business model. However, we did know that he was launching another brand, and these purchases were larger than his typical ones. While I can see how we made the mistake, a deeper look at how we can best serve our clients showed a value that we were missing. We weren't exhibiting the professional curiosity needed to really serve our clients well. There's a fine line between being nosy and being a pest, asking about every financial transaction, and being curious to understand at a deep enough level that you get things right. As a team, we discussed that line and made a conscious choice that struck at the old taboo and made it acceptable for us to be professionally "nosy." As a result, the value of "inquiring" was born at bookskeep, and we established that it was acceptable to question and dig for more information in order to serve our clients well.

As I write this, I know we're living that value! One of our team members, Jessica, sent out a chat explaining that she had a fun call with her client first thing this morning. She called to let him know that when she was working last night around midnight, she found $97,000 dollars in his account at Amazon that had been growing for four years! I asked her to explain how she found it. She explained that she had wanted access to his account for many months and once she got it, she clicked into his main account to ensure that she had the permissions she needed to access his accounting information.

Jessica told me, "All was good in his main account, and I noticed he had signed up for Amazon Pay in addition to his FBA (Fulfillment by Amazon) account. When I clicked into that portal, the page showed a $97,000 account balance and a 'No Bank Account Connected' warning. My heart raced because I had seen this before. With a previous client, I had found $20,000 and, when I called her to check into it, we realized that she had assumed these funds were going into her FBA account and in fact she now had access to $20,000 she didn't know she had. It's like finding money you left in your pocket when you first put on your winter coat in the fall! I knew I made a difference for this client! We both ended up crying on the phone because she shared that her husband had just lost his job, and this was a lifeline. I thought of all of that when I found that $97,000 and, even though it was midnight, I woke my husband up to tell him. When I called my client in the morning, he, in his chill way, said, 'You should have called me last night!'"

I love how Jessica's professional nosiness is rewarded and so do our clients. She had fun sharing the story on chat. Later, I interviewed her for a blog post, and she did a tutorial for the team on how to look for this in their clients' accounts. The inquiring value is connected to caring is connected to educating is connected to gratitude, and so on. I love that we're living that value now!

BUSINESS MODEL AND ALIGNMENT

In addition to values, you also will set your organization's structure, staffing, location, niche, product offering, pricing, and a million other things that will make your business unique to you. Don't let this scare you—and don't assume that the answer to every question is based on how it has always been done before. For example, my reason for starting the business was lifestyle flexibility, so that became a value and ultimately guided my hiring decisions and location. Dave and I worked in our home, staff worked in their homes, we all met clients over video conference, and there was never a need for a physical location. It would have been inconsistent with our values to drive to an office and have staff drive there, and since our clients are all over the world, they weren't going to show up anyway. Your own values and customers will drive a different set of answers based on what you and your clients need.

How you organize your staff to achieve work is also your call. How much do you want to scale? What type of organizational structure will facilitate that growth? My firm went through a period when every bookkeeper reported to one accountant. As we grew, this system became unwieldy. We realized that the organization needed teams to support each other and that one person couldn't have all the answers to every question without it being overwhelming to manage.

We identified team members who were experienced and had strong skills and asked them to serve in a couple of new roles. First, they became the "answer desk" and are on an open call for team members for an hour each day, "The Power Hour." Next, we created monthly training sessions to dive into new technology, refine skills, or improve processes.

Finally, we formed two teams in which members rotate the role of team leader. The team leaders are responsible for preparing an agenda and leading the weekly meetings. In addition, each team has a mentor. Mentors have been with bookskeep for a longer period and have more experience. They are able to help with issues that may come up for the team. The mentors also talk to each other and to the bookskeep leadership team to ensure that teams take advantage of any opportunities to share learning. If there is confusion or a question about business direction or a new process, it is addressed, not left unresolved.

All these structures and educational forums evolved. They weren't necessary at the beginning. Trust yourself to hire according to a fit with your values—and, of course, competency—and let the organizational structure develop to solve needs as they arise. You may require more of a hierarchal structure, or perhaps the team structure will work for you. There are so many variables that impact that decision.

As you grow, understand your True Vision and your values and let them drive many of these organizational decisions. You don't have to have it all figured out right now, and you don't have to assume that it will be the same for you as it is for others. Trust that you will do what is right for your business based on your unique values and culture. If you protect those, you will create the business of your dreams!

For example, Sharon, the CPA and mom from Canada who took a year of maternity leave, also shared with me that she was once faced with the potential loss of a long-time employee who was moving out of the area. "She would come into the office and work occasionally, but over the summer, they moved," Sharon said. "She didn't have to stop being an employee because she works remotely now. Being flexible, and remote work, meant that I didn't lose an employee and she didn't lose her job. She didn't have to go search for a new job in the place where she is now. This decision gave me flexibility in my business and in her business and personal life; we both won!"

You may think, *That's great, but my business wouldn't allow for that.* Each business is unique. Consider what you desire from life and your mothering relationship as you design your business.

I've told you about Julie, the periodontist from Topeka, and her daughter Rachel. You would think a professional with a surgery schedule and office hours would not have much flexibility, but she designed her day so that she would.

"I redid my schedule," Julie explained. "We start at 7:30 a.m. and end at 3:00 p.m. My plan was always to find a before-school place for her to go so I could pick her up. I wanted to be the mom that picked up. I wanted to be the mom that if kids wanted to come to our house or whatever after school, then I would be around. Every one of my staff loves it because they're all moms, too. We get there early, we take a short thirty-minute lunch, and then we're out the door by 3:30 p.m. at the latest. We can be at kids' functions or games, or they're in music lessons or whatever and need to be driven. You know, you become a chauffeur at some point."

In addition to her new hours of operation, Julie introduced block scheduling. "For us, that means we do surgeries in the morning and new patient exams in the afternoon. That way, if one of the new patients doesn't show, we've already got our production for the day because that was in the morning, and that means we can leave a little bit earlier."

You can see that Julie put her lifestyle desires in the driver's seat of her business. In this way, she attracts employees and clients that fit her mode of operation.

Given your own values, you may feel that the traditional growth some businesses try to achieve is not necessarily your growth path. To keep your business and personal life integrated as you desire, you may find it important to regulate how fast you grow your business. When my first book came out, we were blessed with so many leads it was almost crippling. We could have tried to serve them all, quickly added new staff, and strung new clients along as we attempted to keep up, but we knew our reputation would take a hit. We decided to turn away all but the top 10 percent that were potentially the best fit for us to avoid this situation. We limited the number of new clients we could effectively add each month. Once the current month was filled, we started selling the next month, then the next. We typically have work sold one to two months ahead. This has allowed us the time to develop our processes and serve our clients. Now, two years later, we have solid processes and are starting to train additional team members so we can raise that number of new clients.

Your values will guide you as you take on new opportunities and make decisions about creating new products or services. As I wrote this book, I spent a lot of time thinking about my priorities and how to make sure that I kept them front and center. Thinking about my obituary and how I want my daughter to view me as a mom (Chapter 4 exercises) helped me sort through those priorities. I started to consider how this book would enter the world and serve readers—serve you.

Originally, I envisioned starting a coaching business to support women who want to create a business in harmony with their values around mothering and family. Then, out of nowhere, a question hit me: *Is it true that, just because I am very passionate about this topic, I have to build a business to help get it out into the world?* Pondering this question halted my forward progress. I had been working at my desk, preparing for a Profit First mastermind group planning retreat. We had a process, and I was moving through it at a good pace, cranking out the spreadsheets and answering all the questions because I already knew the answers. Suddenly, I didn't know the answers. In fact, I had more questions than answers.

I was progressing down a path that would allow me to sell the business in ten years. All my plans were about scaling and positioning the company for that sale and our retirement, which was now on the planning horizon. It's an intense effort to grow a seven-figure business into a multi-seven-figure business. It requires strategic thought, research, and team growth.

A flood of questions came rushing into my mind. *Could I be in a start-up mindset for one business and a growth mindset for another? What would that divided attention do to my sanity, my peace of mind?* As I've said before, I'm a focus girl, not a multitasking queen. *Could I do both and give them the attention they deserve? Would I still love my life as much as I do now?*

I leaned back in my chair as the thoughts took over. My hands stilled. These were deep questions, questions that required I reexamine my assumptions.

The more I thought about it, the more I realized that the answer was obvious: *This won't work for you!*

Admitting to myself that I should stop and reexamine my assumptions allowed me to look at starting a coaching business from a new perspective. These days, I'm too far removed from the day-to-day of parenting. While I'm empathetic and supportive of my staff with young children, I'm not in the trenches anymore. I have wisdom to share, but my dreams for moms—my dreams for *you*—could be best fulfilled by writing this book and then letting someone else take the lead.

There's always more than one way to achieve your dreams, and not all of them require the same amount of effort. As I've encouraged you to do throughout this book, you can do things your way. Then, as things change, you can alter your course and do things a different way (that is still your way). I loved being a mom and starting a business from scratch, but that didn't mean I had to repeat the process.

As I let go of my assumption that I had to be the one to help readers find their way after they read this book, I knew I had to find a special person to take its ideas into the world. More than anything, I wanted you to have a community to help you chart your course. I was considering how to find that unicorn person when, suddenly, she appeared.

While I was editing for this book, I sent out advance copies to ideal readers along with a set of nine questions. Almost everyone answered the questions in very helpful short paragraphs—everyone except Julia. She sent me three pages of the most exquisite feedback that was so insightful, it was as if she were in my own mind. I asked her if we could chat.

It wasn't long before I saw that Julia was the right person to lead this effort. We started with her helping me refine the exercises. Then I realized she wasn't refining; she was redesigning them to make them better. We discussed the business she might create to support moms who want to start or grow their businesses. As my licensee, Julia has helped make this book more useful to moms with her Acorn Mom community and programs (acornmom.com). The decision to step back so I could live the life I envisioned and still realize this dream of helping moms allowed me to keep moving forward in alignment with my values, goals, and True Vision.

Just as when you start your business, you want to grow your business in context and alignment with your overall personal and business goals. You are the center of the family you're creating; your values are the center of the business you're creating. That means they will be living and changing, but their impermanence doesn't diminish their importance. Of all the things on your list every day, mindset and values should not be pushed aside or buried. They are the foundational work. Having the Sacred Space to work on them is crucial as you are faced with and overcome the challenges that are part of parenting and business ownership. Take a few minutes now to get started on this important work.

CREATE AND DECLARE BUSINESS VALUES

Suggested Time to Complete: This exercise could take one to three hour-long meetings if you are working with your team. If you are doing this on your own, set aside ninety minutes.

⊘ **When you complete this exercise,** you will have guiding values that are easy to live and apply in daily operations.

⊗ **If you skip this exercise**, your business may grow in a way that is outside of your vision and in conflict with your personal values.

- Start with your personal values, which are the core of this process (and this book). They are not separate from your business; they are its driving force. List your primary personal values. Limit this list to the big three.
- Now, look at the list and consider your team (or the team you want to have someday). Are you missing a key value that would help you support them?
- Next, consider your customers. What values will help you attract and keep them? Add these values to your list. Remember, your business value list is different from your Immutable Laws, which are about the lines your business does not cross.
- Finally, consider how your values will help guide you and your team to serve, make decisions, interact with people, and run things on a daily basis. Looking at each value on your list, what are five behaviors you and/or your team could engage in that demonstrate those values?
- Once you've completed this process, follow Jesse Cole's lead and put your values in alphabetical order so you can easily remember them.

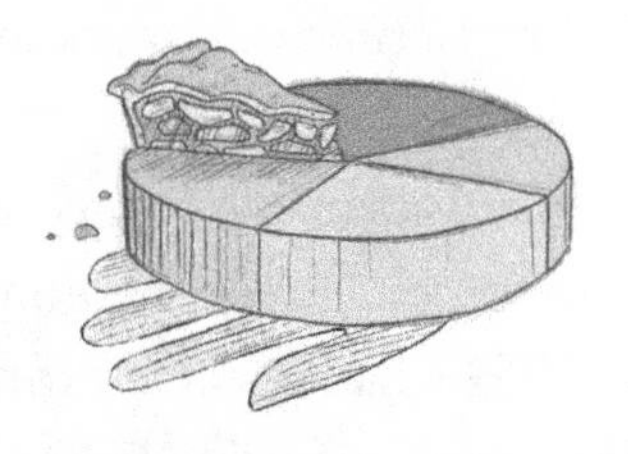

CHAPTER 9

WHEN THINGS DON'T GO AS PLANNED

MARA IS A FORCE OF nature. She has a PhD in geophysics and had a career in that field for ten years. Then she switched her focus and became a software engineer. She was a manager at the software firm when she had her two children. Mara chose to have children on her own through donor conception. She knew she would be juggling many roles as a new parent, so she moved into planning mode. But sometimes, things don't go as planned.

"With my first child, I planned it all out when I was about three months pregnant," Mara told me. "I made a proposal and turned it in to my boss. I would take twelve to thirteen weeks of leave, which they were offering, and another thirteen weeks at 60 percent time. The next six months I would work at 80 percent until my child was a year old. It was also important to me that I maintain two weeks of vacation time in my vacation bank to ensure I could take time off for doctor appointments, sick child days, etc.

"My boss approved this plan and turned it in to HR, and I waited for five months. When I was eight months pregnant, my boss told me the VP of HR had rejected my proposal because I was a manager. They were not going to allow me to be part-time beyond the six-month mark. They gave me three months part-time after my maternity leave ended, but they didn't want to give me the extra six months part-time. I was devastated and I was hormonal. I had a really supportive boss, and he said, 'I'll be as flexible as you need me to be.' I adjusted my schedule as I needed to, and I got paid full-time and worked more than full-time, but I got the ability to rearrange my work schedule as needed for my family."

Mara made a plan that fit her unique situation and, while her proposal was not approved, she did get flexibility, which is what she really wanted. She made a similar pitch when she was pregnant with her second child.

Mara's planning served her well; her second child survived a stroke near the time of birth. Parenting a stroke survivor became a third job. She explains, "There was my software engineering manager job, my mom role, and the role of caring for and advocating for my stroke survivor, frequently driving an hour into Boston for appointments that took half the day." Each trip meant using vacation time, which she had set aside.

Sometimes, no matter how carefully we plan and consider the next steps, life throws us off course. And sometimes, in order to build the life we want, we have to make adjustments we didn't expect—or want—to make. In this chapter, I'll share some stories from moms who are business owners and how they navigated unexpected bumps in the road.

TAKE THE TIME YOU NEED TO TRANSITION

Mara has specific training that makes her uniquely suited to parent a stroke survivor. She is passionate in her hobby practice of the Feldenkrais Method®, an approach to neuromuscular education that brings awareness and possibility into all aspects of your life.

"I was completely fascinated by watching my kids develop. I was very engrossed and happy. I felt needed and able to help my child with the brain injury because of my training in this method. Eleven years ago, I wanted to quit my job and start my business helping children as a Feldenkrais Method® practitioner, but financially, I just couldn't see how to do it then. I was quite terrified, actually, about being a single mom and starting a business from scratch."

Mara ultimately took the leap to develop her business three years ago. Work had become so stressful that she developed a stress-related physical illness. After three years of on-and-off medical leave periods, she decided that she needed a sabbatical and to self-fund her time off. Rather than look at her situation and determine her next steps "forever," she initially gave herself a year to work through the transition. She calculated her financial runway and knew that she and her children would be okay for a year.

For that year, she focused on her passion. At the end of it, she had come through well enough to give herself another year.

And when that year was up, she gave herself another. Finally, she decided to leave her job altogether.

Today, Mara no longer feels terrified of the double role of single mom and entrepreneur. She has had time with her children without the demands of a job that was so stressful she was physically ill from work. She is poised for her business to take off, and her financial runway continues to hold up.

Mara's strategy of giving herself a year of transition allowed her to move forward with intention and focus. "I'm still trying to feel secure in my footing, but it's like, I know that I'm on the path that I'm meant to be on. It's not just a someday career. It's a passion. My five-year and my ten-year visions are crystal clear. I'm in the first three years and I'm still in transition."

Mara and I talked about how her sabbatical was, in effect, a mind game she played with herself. I think it provides a useful framework for us to think about our own endeavors. So often, we have expectations about where we will be at a certain point in time or after a certain amount of effort. Taking a sabbatical to start her business gave Mara the freedom to focus on her future plan and not stress about a fallback plan. She wasn't putting herself out there halfheartedly and dividing her attention by doing her business development while simultaneously searching for a job. She made a commitment to a path for a certain period knowing that if it didn't work, there was another path she could take. Mara shared with me that she had used this technique before while finishing her postdoc. At that time, she was in a new job with a defense contractor that she didn't enjoy. When she encountered friends and family, they would ask her how she liked it. She didn't want to say she hated it in response, so she gave herself a year of transition.

She would answer her friends truthfully, saying, "I'm in transition. I'm going to wait a year and then I'll decide." By the end of that year, she had an opportunity to move into the software field and she exited into another position and another career path.

If you're stressing about an outcome, give yourself time to be in transition. Taking the pressure off allows you to see things more clearly, and being open allows you to attract the kinds of opportunities you desire.

ASK FOR SUPPORT TO CARRY YOU THROUGH

As we learned from Mara, things don't always go according to plan. However, things can work out if you are open to change and have confidence that the best options will present themselves as you need them. Sometimes transitions are thrust upon us. When I interviewed Julie and Sharon, I learned how they developed their businesses and managed some unexpected circumstances. Both received an unusual level of support from their former bosses.

Julie is a periodontist. Before her now-teenage daughter was born, Julie was working for a dentist with the understanding that she would buy his practice in two years. She gained vital experience working under him, learning the business side of things that they didn't teach her in dental school. During this time, Julie took a seven-week maternity leave to have her daughter, Rachel. Everything lined up as planned for the business purchase. Julie attended a dental conference out of town and Rachel, six months old, stayed with Julie's mom.

Julie remembers, "My mom was watching my daughter and Rachel started having seizures. They thought it might be fever-related, but it ended up being a much bigger deal. We headed home and as soon as we landed, my mom called and said, 'Come to the ER now.' We got in the car and drove down.

"Rachel ended up in the hospital for ten days. We didn't know what was going on. We didn't know if it was meningitis, if it was viral or bacterial, so they had to treat her for both. We didn't know how serious it was because she didn't really act sick."

Julie and her boss were supposed to close on the business during this time, but since she was in the hospital with Rachel, the business purchase got pushed back.

"Here I am, my baby is really sick, we don't know what's wrong, and I'm supposed to be buying this business and I'm freaking out. You remember what it's like when you have a little baby that gets sick, it's like, all the time. I couldn't be off much and my (now ex) husband was a teacher at the time, so he had a little flexibility, but not much. Neither of us needed to miss work to take her to doctor's appointments and all that. Thankfully, the previous owner agreed to stay on as my associate for two years. He was planning to retire, but he worked part-time and helped cover, which was good."

Sharon, the CPA from Canada, had support from her former boss, too. She left for a year of maternity leave, expecting to return and become a partner in the firm. However, when she returned, the owner of the firm explained that he no longer wanted to take additional partners into the firm.

"He didn't want to let me go, but he didn't want a partner," Sharon explained. "So he allowed me to build my own firm while I was employed there. He was very supportive and I was able to build my business alongside working for him. My kids were both in a daycare home full-time. I built my business mostly in the evenings after the kids went to bed and on weekends. It was really slow to get established. I worked until I was sure I had enough revenue to make it. Then I left the job. But I still work in the office, and he rents me office space."

As moms, we are typically responsible people, which spills over into our work. Mara, Julie, and Sharon all made plans about how to handle their work after maternity leave, but situations changed for them. When work plans don't go as hoped or your child has challenges, you will rise to the occasion and find a solution that works for all. You will do this because you are a mom, and moms are responsible, resilient problem-solvers. Go into your role as a business owner with your eyes open to uncertainty and your heart and head primed to respond with flexibility and possibility, and you'll manage with grace.

LET GO OF BELIEFS THAT NO LONGER SERVE YOU

FEMKE WAS ALREADY A SUCCESSFUL business owner when she began to think about children. You might recall her story from earlier in the book. She is the owner and official licensee of Profit First Professionals in the Netherlands.

Femke was an interim financial controller working as a consultant when she realized that she wanted to have children, but she didn't get pregnant right away. She remembers saying to her husband, "I have just enough work to be a mother. There is room now to have children, so where are they?"

Femke and her husband Bart didn't have to wait much longer. They are now the parents of two young boys.

Fiercely independent in a way I've not seen amongst my friends in the US, Femke told me how concerned she was about finances when she got pregnant. "Bart and I decided that temporarily I should pay less [to their household expenses], and it freaked me out completely!" Femke remembers her father saying to her when she was a child, "Stand on your own legs. Don't be dependent on anyone." She wanted a child, but she believed that she should not be dependent on Bart in any way. To realize her dream of having a child, she had to let go of that belief and allow Bart to chip in more financially. The transition from equal to unequal financial contributor was temporary.

She and Bart worked it out and she stepped back her financial contribution with the birth of their first son. In turn, Bart stepped up in many ways. He also took family leave and cut back his working hours. Femke worked three days a week; Bart took every Friday off and the boys went to a family-type daycare two days a week. Bart's employer extended his leave long-term, and today he still works this schedule so he can have time with his now eight- and nine-year-old boys.

After their boys were born, Femke transitioned again. She grew her business deliberately in a way that aligns with her parenting. While the boys are at school, she schedules the components she loves: education, speaking, and being an ambassador for small business success. She leaves the day-to-day operations to her manager. Femke now is the high earner in the family and relishes the independence. She didn't start there. She evolved.

PROGRESS NUGGET: *"It is only because of problems that we grow mentally and spiritually."*
—M. Scott Peck[34]

DO WHAT'S BEST FOR YOU

As moms and business owners, it is so easy for us to get caught up in comparisons. In part, we want some validation that we're on the right path. In some instances, we're competitive. I can tell you, though, that comparisons will make you crazy. Even more than that, they will take your focus away from what is important for you, your family, and your business. Family members share their opinions to be helpful. Social media groups that could build you up as a mom or business owner can end up being hurtful. While I've recommended a support network and accountability groups, make sure that the communities you participate in really do feed your spirit and that their mission is to serve and present what is best for you.

In Chapter 5, I shared Tracy's story. She is mom to Lance, who needed extra help with executive functioning. When she needed more of a community around parenting than her circle of friends, she turned to online "mommy groups." But what she found was far from the support she needed.

"The mommy wars are alive and well in these groups," Tracy said. "I would try to be a part of those communities and there were so many arguments about circumcising or breastfeeding or sleep training, opinions about child-raising in general. There's just a lot of external stuff that I tend to internalize."

Tracy also identified an issue that I heard about from several mothers. She realized that she's in a small subset of business owner moms and it's hard to find each other. "There are moms who stay at home and moms who have jobs. They are more typical than those who own businesses, like me. It is a completely different animal, like having a job *and* having a business; it's a whole different thing, and it impacts your parenting."

Wendy—the accountant from South Africa who started a business, went back to work, then started a business again—had a similar experience. "I think the hardest part for me of balancing being a business owner and a mom, which both take so much time and energy, is that I don't have the friendship circle of girlfriends that I used to have," she said. "I miss that and it is the trade-off right now. I also think being self-employed adds another dynamic to it, in that some girlfriends have nine-to-five jobs. Our conversations just don't jibe. Their life is about cooking and recipes because they work from nine to five. But then when they get home, it's all about what TV they watch and what they're cooking for dinner. And we don't really have much to talk about because for me, my job never ends. I mean, yes, I'm home for dinner, but I don't lie around watching TV. If I am watching TV, my brain is going over my to-do list for tomorrow and thinking about who I didn't call that I should have called and the conversation I should have had. I found that narrows the friend pool even more, because my best friends are going to be people I can collaborate with. That's why the Profit First network has been so great—it's people in the same place that I am."

It's important to find a supportive community of other moms where you can be yourself. A community made up of moms who are business owners, where you can find people who deal with the same issues you face. A community that does not engage in the comparison or guilt game, where you can "do you" and be you. You can find that community of supportive, like-minded women on the Acorn Mom platform that Julia developed. Acorn Mom helps mothers and caregivers unlock their entrepreneurial potential. In addition to a community that will help lift you up, Acorn Mom offers courses and coaching to help you implement and expand on the concepts covered in in this book. Connect with Acorn Mom at AcornMom.com or by scanning this QR code.

As a periodontist, Julie's business requires her to be hands-on. She schedules her surgeries in the morning, and she can't delegate those to her team. She realized when Rachel went to school that she had to let go of the idea that she was going to be the mom who was always there for the class parties and trips. Julie describes it like this.

"You know, if you're trying to compare yourself to a mom who doesn't work outside of the home, it's just not the same. And it's okay if they're totally different. She's not trying to juggle the same kind of balls I'm trying to juggle. And she's going to be able to pick up some slack that I can't, but I'm going to be better at some other things, too. But you know, we moms never remember the things that our kids are learning by us being business owners. Instead, as moms, we focus on 'I'm not there.'"

What Julie points out is gold. We focus on what we're not doing, not what we actually do. This is human nature, but we can learn a new practice that will help with this negative mindset. It is simple to make a daily practice of spending some time focusing on the things we are grateful for. One of my values in my business is gratitude. We practice gratitude because it keeps our focus on what is, not what isn't.

Wendy shared that being a parent and a mom makes her feel grateful. She added, "When I am with my children at 3:30 in the afternoon, roller-skating in the park, I feel intense gratitude for the life that I've chosen for myself. And when I'm working with clients and my children are at school or with their dad, I have intense gratitude for being able to do the work I love. Having both, I think it's not about better or worse or pass or fail. I think it's about gratitude that I get to do both.

"I am a professional. I have a career I'm proud of. And I am also willing to get dirty and build Legos on the floor with them, as opposed to my mother, who I love dearly, who only had one role. And that was to be my mom. She did a great job at it, but there was always this piece of me that looked at her and said, *This is your job? Like, making sandwiches every day and being at school, that's your job? Don't you want more?* And that's just me. I was always, *Don't you want more?* I'm really proud to be able to show my children that you can have both, if you choose."

Sharon sums it up very succinctly. When it comes to being a mom, "Do what you think works best for your family and don't let distractions or what other people might think influence your decisions. Focus on what works for you and just do that."

TAKE THE FIRST STEP

As you can see, there is no one way to do pregnancy, maternity leave, motherhood or small business ownership. That is what makes this entire scenario of mom and business owner so perfect: You get to do both your way. And you don't have to have all the answers right now. Sure, make a plan and work the plan, but be prepared for things unfold differently. Your baby may have health challenges, like Mara and Julie's children did. There will be a way to make it work, just as they did. Don't let the possible issues stop you. If you've built your support team, you'll be fine. The same is true on the business side of things. There will always be challenges, and you will figure them out. The cool thing is, you get to create the business using your compass. Setting the direction and aligning the values allows you the opportunity to create a culture that not only accommodates motherhood, but celebrates it.

I didn't have all the answers before I started my business. The women I interviewed for this book didn't, either. What they all had was a mindset to grow. Guess what? You've already got that mindset, or you wouldn't have picked up this book in the first place, and you certainly wouldn't have made it to the end. I have shared experiences and strategies to help you realize that you're not alone, that there are multiple ways to move forward no matter where you get stuck, and that you have what it takes to be successful. My intention is to boost your confidence to take the first step and help you realize it's not a race. The journey is really the fun part, so enjoy the ride.

That first step will also look different depending on where you are with your pregnancy, motherhood, and your business idea. All journeys start out as a dream. Once we are pregnant, we monitor our progress in terms of trimesters. If you're already a mom, you realize that there is no real time definition around pregnancy that makes sense. From my research, a trimester can be twelve or thirteen weeks. Which is it? I'm an accountant and I know weeks matter; don't the doctors have this figured out by now?! But then again, the conventional wisdom is that you're pregnant for nine months, which is really forty weeks, which feels more like ten months. If we think about trimesters as thirteen weeks, we see that the same timing construct exists in business; a period of thirteen weeks happens to be a quarter of the calendar year in the business world. We do quarterly planning, and financial results are reported quarterly. Isn't it interesting how the big cycles in life, like seasons and giving birth, also follow us in business? See? You've got this. You've been participating in the game of life, well, your whole life!

Maybe you're wondering, when do I start? The answer is now! And where do I start? Pick your path. If you've worked on the exercises, you've already started. If not, then go back through them and pick one that feels easy for you. After you complete one, pick the next one that may be slightly harder. These exercises are part of a deliberate process to help you develop this new mindset.

If you skipped the exercises altogether, or if you think you need a visible reminder to help you throughout the day, then write down the three sentences below and tape them where you will see them. Think about them during your day-to-day activities. You might post them on the bathroom mirror, the refrigerator, and your computer screen. These questions are a way to keep your new mindset front and center.

As a mom and businesses owner, I will do ______ today.

As a mom and business owner, I will NOT do ______ today.

As a mom and business owner, this is the last time I will do ______.

Every day, as you make your daily plans, consider these statements. As you contemplate the to-do list, what small step, what one thing are you going to do to move yourself in the direction you want to go? Don't worry if it's not perfect. Any movement is a chance to learn, and just setting this context will move you forward on your journey.

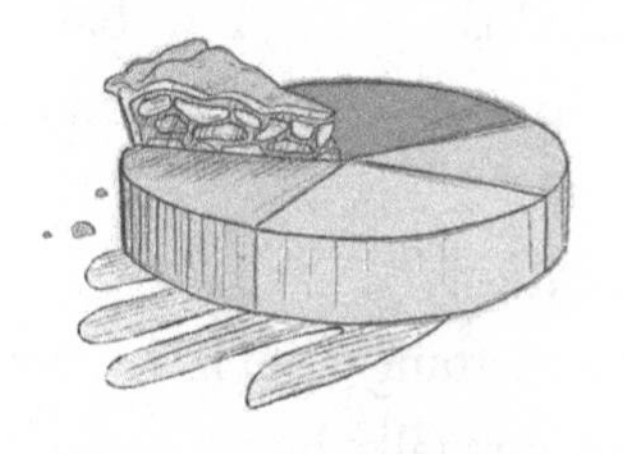

CHAPTER 10

LEARNING TO FLY

You're full of it. This was my thought after I got off my monthly coaching call with Mike Michalowicz. He had asked me to do something I knew would never happen. Never.

Our goal that day had been to prepare for a sales call I had coming up the following day. My aim was to sell my prospective client on my skills as an ecommerce accountant and ask for a contract that was twice as large as any I had ever presented. The contract was for a typical amount of work, but the increased price was because I was now an expert and commanded more in the marketplace.

When Mike suggested I nearly double my fees, I truly thought he was feeding me a line.

Perhaps he could sense I was laughing at him in my own mind, because he said, "You're the Profit First expert in ecommerce, right? You see that, right?"

That's a stretch, I thought. I had been working with ecommerce clients for about six months. Experts have more time in the trenches, right? Except… I probably *did* know more than anyone else about applying Profit First to ecommerce businesses.

Hmm. Maybe someday.

Then Mike said something that I knew would never happen, no matter how many pep talks he gave me: "Are you prepared to take the stage at ecommerce conferences and help these business owners learn how to be profitable?"

I knew he wanted me to say yes, so I said, "Yeah, sure."

But I was thinking, *Yeah, right.* That *ain't gonna happen.*

In my corporate career, I started as a receptionist and left fourteen years later as a senior vice president. My role was behind the scenes. My boss handled all the public-facing and speaking opportunities. I never allowed myself to think about being the frontwoman. I knew how to make the office hum, how to bring in new business, and how to build relationships with the electric utilities and the electric utility commission in the state of North Carolina. I had nothing to say from the podium; that wasn't my interest, and fortunately, my boss had it covered.

Though I doubted Mike's confidence in me, I put on my best acting face for my call with my prospect and delivered that offer the next day. I had to hold myself together when the client accepted it. *Wow. This guy is easily fooled.*

I was also afraid that I was going to be "found out" soon. The client told me he had been using a retired accountant who was a former partner with Arthur Andersen when it was a Big Five accounting firm. I just knew this guy had tricks up his sleeve that were created before I was even born. The imposter syndrome insecurities really set in.

Within a couple of days, I received access to my new client's QuickBooks account and was astounded by what I saw. The bookkeeping was a total disaster—epic, biblical-scale disaster. But, while the books were a mess, I was so excited because I knew how to clean them up. I created a chart of accounts that showed my client how much money he was making from various ecommerce platforms. It also showed his costs so we could calculate gross and net margins. His books told a story, and I brought that story to light.

About a month later, I presented this new set of books to my client. After answering his questions, seeing his acknowledgment of information he could use to make decisions, and presenting a Profit First assessment that would become the baseline for our work going forward, a new thought popped into my mind.

I am the Profit First Ecommerce expert!

As I gained confidence in my role as expert over the following months, that coaching call with Mike still played over in my mind. I had been so sure he was wrong, that I would never take the stage to speak about Profit First. And yet I had landed the client I thought would never pay me the increased price, served him well, and come to believe I really was *the* Profit First professional who knew the most about ecommerce.

Why are you holding yourself back? I thought about that day I mentioned in the introduction to this book, when I surprised myself by standing up in the boardroom and advocating for the program we created. Even though some perceived the points I made as "motherhood, apple pie, and all that happy horseshit," I knew better. Then I thought about how I had designed a business that served my life, that allowed me to be the mother

I wanted to be. When I started, I had no idea how to do that; I simply took the first step and let my personal values guide me. Maybe I *could* come out from behind the curtain and take the stage. I could take the first step…

In the years that followed, I took step after step and took "the stage" over and over again. I wrote the bestselling Profit First derivative, *Profit First for Ecommerce Sellers,* which still sells about fifteen copies each day. I have presented at some of the largest and most respected ecommerce conferences, such as ASD (Affordable Shopping Destination) Market Week, Amazing's SellerCon, Prosper, and others. I've appeared on hundreds of podcasts.

In his book, *Fix This Next,* Mike shares a story about keynoting at a conference, something he does dozens of times a year. He had popped into the room to catch part of another speech and get a feel for the room. The person seated beside him introduced himself and inquired about Mike's line of work. Mike shared that he had a small business. Then his seatmate said, "You should read this book, *Profit First*. It really helped me in my business." Mike started to come clean and say that he was, in fact, the author of that book, but before he could say anything, his seatmate added, "Look it up; it's by Cyndi Thomason." What an honor to be confused with my mentor Mike Michalowicz![35] I had been so reluctant to see myself as the expert in applying Profit First for ecommerce, and now this person thought of me as the author of the original book!

Meanwhile, the client I presented to all those years ago is still doing well. In sharing his most recent year-end financial reports, I congratulated him on his success and recapped how his business had grown during our years together. He wrote me back the nicest short note that read: "It's been a wild ride. Thanks for being a big part of my success and helping me set the foundation to understand how a business operates!" It's always nice to get a heartfelt thank you, but I especially love this because he appreciated me for my educating value.

The reason I share this story is not to shine a light on my accomplishments; it's to help you see that when I started out, I didn't have confidence or a grand plan. I didn't believe that I would step out on a stage or write one book, let alone two. I simply put one foot in front of the other by doing what seemed right at the time, with my personal values as my touchstone. I ask for and receive lots of professional help from people who have "been there" and "done that" before me and are willing to share their expertise. I have support from my family and friends when I need it. I have wonderful employees who care deeply for each other and our clients.

If you've approached this book and these exercises with skepticism, I get it. You can see that along the way, I did that with my mentors, too. While I truly believe that the stories and exercises in this book will help you move forward and give you a few shortcuts that helped me and my colleagues, I know the most important thing is that you take action and just start. Even though you have no idea where it will lead, start. If the ideas you come up with scare you to death, start anyway. If you feel like an imposter, do the work and become the expert.

You may not see the whole path ahead of you, but one of the most important lessons I've learned is that having faith in your ability to recognize what is right and what to do next is all you need. When I'm taking the stage to speak, I envision that someone in my audience needs what I have to share. I ask the divine to help me be of service with my presentation. I look at everyone in the audience and know they are there to boost me up. The edge of the stage does not drop off onto a cliff. Instead, in my mind, I step onto a bridge. That bridge is the audience, made up of individual people who are there to learn and grow. If I can have that level of confidence in total strangers, I am sure you have people in your life who are the bridge of support for you.

When you start and take those first steps, know that these tips and tools are here for you to make the journey a little easier. I'm so excited to see what you do now to create your dream life. You deserve it, your children deserve it, your clients deserve it, and society needs you to take care of those around you as only you can.

You might remember the pivotal conversation Dave and I had on our way to the airport, when we decided to change everything and design our work life to have a family. Twenty-three years later, we were in the car again—this time coming home from the airport, where we had picked up our daughter, Alaina. She had just wrapped up her yearlong service program with FEMA Americorps. She'd been interested in disaster relief and decided that this program was a way to learn more about it and possibly work with FEMA itself later if she liked the work.

I took advantage of the time we had in the car together to learn about her plans and how my decisions in parenting had impacted her. Specifically, I asked, "Do you think anything that you observed with me being a business owner influenced what you want to do with your life?"

"I don't want to be particularly beholden to anyone because I like seeing how free you are with your job," Alaina said. "I also realize how stressful it is not having a bigger business above you because you're responsible for your own success and failures. That's really stressful to me, and I think that I want to do what I'm doing for a while longer, that is, working for a bigger business. That way I can prepare myself more if I decide to go for my own business, because I realize the consequences that could happen."

Alaina told me about her plans to finish school and work as a reservist for FEMA, and to respond to disasters whenever and however they happen. She had it all figured out: She would get a degree in emergency management so she could travel and do the hands-on work she enjoys.

Wow. She knew what she wanted, and she knew she could design it. What more could a mother ask for?

Then Alaina said, "I grew up with a mindset that, you know, the women in our family could do well at whatever they wanted to do. It was very clear to me that you being a stay-at-home mom was a choice and something that you sacrificed a lot for. It was a very good demonstration that the women in our family are badass and that we can do whatever the hell we want."

You are designing a work and family life that suits your needs and desires and is driven by your personal values. This will give you the life you want. But more than that, it will give your children the *example* that *they,* too, can design the life they want. Imagine—you're creating a new legacy for your children, and their children, and so on. A legacy of creating a life, rather than letting it happen to you. A legacy of considering and honoring all aspects of life, not just work and money. A legacy of doing what it takes to live the life of your dreams.

Take the first step. Let your personal values guide you.

Take another step. The tools and resources are there for you.

Take the next step, and the next step, and the next step. The bridge will be there when you need it.

Don't look back. Don't look down. Just take that step and fly.

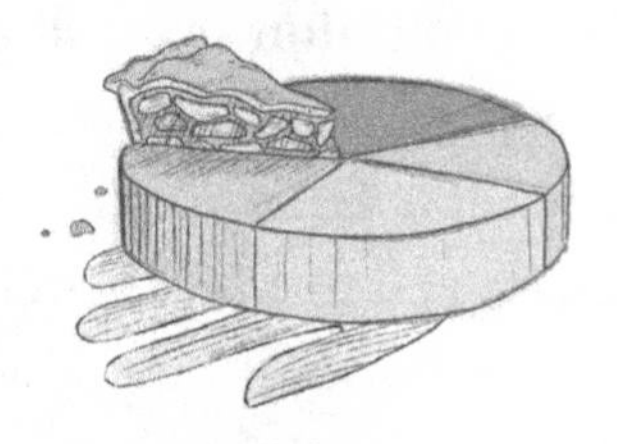

ACKNOWLEDGMENTS

THIS BOOK EXISTS BECAUSE GENEROUS moms shared their stories. Thank you, AJ, Alicia, Femke, Julia, Julie, Kasey, Laura, Mara, Sharon, Susanne, Tracy, and Wendy, for your willingness to tell the stories of what you learned about yourselves, your families, and your businesses. I know that our readers will connect with your experience and benefit from your example. Each of you are making your own hero's journey, and your children, your employees, your clients, and the world will be changed because of your efforts and your hearts.

Thank you to Dave, Alaina, and Eleanor, my mom, for being my support system and encouraging me to find a way to get this book done—for that matter, to get whatever I'm attempting done. You are always my biggest cheerleaders and I love you for it. Thank you to George, my dad, for teaching me the value of patience and always being so patient with me.

Julia Nardelli Gross, thank you for giving me great advance reader feedback and for jumping on board to help other mom entrepreneurs with the Acorn Mom community. Your passion for our message and your caring and clear direction will help so many moms. Your dedication as we slogged through all the feedback, rewrites, and edits has made this process fun and smoother. And Jeremy Gross, thank you for taking my challenging worksheets and turning them into spreadsheet masterpieces. These are real tools now. The effort you have both given to making the exercises great really will help our readers put the ideas to work with ease.

Thank you, Mike Michalowicz: You gave me the confidence in myself to step into my author skin. Your example and help, no matter the challenge, has been a guiding light for me. You believed in this book before I did. Because of you, I took this book off my ten-year plan and moved it to year one. You knew where my heart was, and I appreciate you holding up the mirror.

To Dr. Bob Koger, my early mentor and boss at AEC/ Advanced Energy: Thank you for having confidence in me and elevating my focus from support to leadership. You changed my identity when you did.

AJ Harper, working with you has given me a glimpse into your pure genius. Your guidance in asking the penetrating questions caused me to reframe challenges from the perspective of my reader and gives my thinking so much more depth. I have learned so much about myself as you helped me edit this book. Thank you, too, for creating the Top Three Book Workshop. The talent in our group inspires me every single day as I participate in writing sprints, live editing events, and Monday Night Readings. You and Laura Stone are steadfast in your support and love for our community, and I am so grateful for you and my friends in Top Three.

Thank you, Zoë Bird, for having my back on the copy edits and making this book better. I'm so glad we could work together again. Thank you, Choi Messer, for getting my message and giving me cover and interior page design that feels like home. Your mom entrepreneur journey is also an inspiration, and I'm thankful that you are sharing your gifts with me on this book. Thank you, John Stephan, of MCS Studios for once again recording the audio version and making the process delightful.

I had wonderful feedback from my advance readers. Thank you so much for your gift of time and insight, Abby Wilson, Beth Fynbo, Carrie Richter, Eleni Paria, Ester Hacken, Julia Nardelli Gross, Maja Donker, Mathea Ford, Louise Pooley, and Tatiana Tsoir.

booksPeeps are my why! I love that each of you make such a great, supportive team and that you look for ways to help each other at work and in your personal lives. I love that you love each other. I am so proud of you and appreciate the way you support me and our clients every day while making your home lives hum.

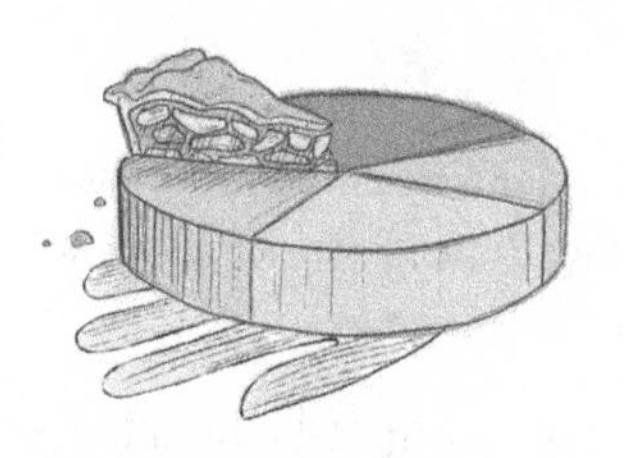

ENDNOTES

Introduction

[1] Philip H. Dougherty, "Advertising: Secrets of Selling to Women," *The New York Times,* Wednesday, October 31, 1979, archived at https://www.nytimes.com/1979/10/31/archives/advertising-secrets-of-selling-to-women.html/, accessed February 10, 2022.

[2] Sheryl Sandberg, *Lean In: Women, Work, and the Will to Lead* (New York, NY: Knopf, 2013).

[3] Susan Adams, "10 Things Sheryl Sandberg Gets Exactly Right in *Lean In,*" Forbes.com, March 4, 2013, https://www.forbes.com/sites/susanadams/2013/03/04/10-things-sheryl-sandberg-gets-exactly-right-in-lean-in/?sh=2ed2dc87ada9, accessed February 10, 2022.

[4] Anne-Marie Slaughter, "Why Women Still Can't Have It All," TheAtlantic.com, July/August 2012 issue, https://www.theatlantic.com/magazine/archive/2012/07/why-women-still-cant-have-it-all/309020/, accessed February 10, 2022.

Chapter 1

[5] Rosamund Stone Zander and Benjamin Zander, *The Art of Possibility: Transforming Professional and Personal Life* (New York, NY: Penguin, 2002).

[6] "Otto Berman," Wikipedia.org, last edited November 22, 2021, https://en.wikipedia.org/wiki/Otto_Berman, accessed February 10, 2022.

[7] Chabeli Carrazana, "865,000 Women Left the Workforce Last Month" USAToday.com, October 11, 2020, https://www.usatoday.com/story/news/politics/2020/10/11/865-000-women-were-laid-off-last-month/3609016001/

Chapter 2

[8] Joseph Campbell, *The Power of Myth* (New York, NY: Anchor, 1991).

[9] Campbell, *Power of Myth*

[10] Campbell, *Power of Myth*

Chapter 3

[11] Michelle Obama, *Becoming* (New York, NY: Crown, 2018).

Chapter 4

[12] Mike Michalowicz, *Profit First: Transforming Your Business from a Cash-Eating Monster to a Money-Making Machine* (New York, NY: Portfolio, 2017).

[13] Richard Scarry, *What Do People Do All Day?* (New York, NY: Random House, 1968).

[14] LegalZoom Staff, "86 Key Entrepreneur Statistics for 2021 and Beyond," LegalZoom.com, July 14, 2021, https://www.legalzoom.com/articles/entrepreneur-statistics, accessed February 10, 2022.

Chapter 5

[15] Stephen R. Covey: *The 7 Habits of Highly Successful People: Powerful Lessons in Personal Change* (New York, NY: Free Press, 1989).

[16] James Allen, *As a Man Thinketh,* 1902.

[17] Shel Silverstein, *The Giving Tree* (New York, NY: Harper Collins, 1964).

[18] Topher Payne, "The Tree Who Set Healthy Boundaries: An Alternate Ending to Shel Silverstein's *The Giving Tree,*" YouTube.com, June 19, 2021, https://www.youtube.com/watch?v=ezH-SnJfxgc, accessed February 10, 2022.

[19] Mike Michalowicz, *The Toilet Paper Entrepreneur: The Tell-It-Like-It-Is Guide to Cleaning Up in Business, Even If You Are at the End of Your Roll* (Boonton, NJ: Obsidian Launch, 2008).

[20] Laurence Sterne Quotes. BrainyQuote.com, BrainyMedia Inc, 2022. https://www.brainyquote.com/quotes/laurence_sterne_165818, accessed February 10, 2022.

[21] Gary Keller and Jay Papasan, *The One Thing: The Surprisingly Simple Truth About Extraordinary Results* (Austin, TX: Bard Press, 2013).

[22] Emily Nagoski and Amelia Nagoski, "The cure for burnout (hint: it isn't self-care)," TED.com, April, 2021, https://www.ted.com/talks/emily_nagoski_and_amelia_nagoski_the_cure_for_burnout_hint_it_isn_t_self_care?language=en, accessed February 10, 2022.

[23] Henry Ford Quotes. BrainyQuote.com, BrainyMedia Inc, 2022. https://www.brainyquote.com/quotes/henry_ford_145978, accessed February 10, 2022.

Chapter 6

[24] Michalowicz, *Profit First*

[25] "Jeanne Calment," Wikipedia.org, last edited February 5, 2022, https://en.wikipedia.org/wiki/Jeanne_Calment, last accessed February 10, 2022.

[26] Brian Dyson, "Coca-Cola CEO's Secret Formula for Success: Vision, Confidence and Luck," commencement speech delivered at Georgia Tech, Sept 6, 1991, MarkTurner.net, May 10, 2015, https://www.markturner.net/2015/05/10/text-of-brian-dysons-commencement-speech-at-georgia-tech-sept-1991/>, accessed February 10, 2022.

[27] Katie Reilly, "Muhammad Ali's Wit and Wisdom: 6 of His Best Quotes," Time.com, June 4, 2016, https://time.com/4357493/muhammad-ali-dead-best-quotes/, accessed February 10, 2022.

[28] Sam Medley, "The average iPhone user spends a full work week on their phone, a new report claims," NotebookCheck.net, 9/20/21, https://www.notebookcheck.net/The-average-iPhone-user-spends-a-full-work-week-on-their-phone-a-new-report-claims.562797.0.html, accessed February 10, 2022.

[29] Caroline Bologna, "23 Times Tina Fey Hilariously Summed Up Parenting," HuffPost.com, May 11, 2021, https://www.huffpost.com/entry/23-times-tina-fey-hilariously-summed-up-parenting_n_591a7d9de4b0809be15797ea, accessed February 10, 2022.

Chapter 7

[30] Michalowicz, *Profit First*

[31] Sigmund Freud, Carl Gustav Jung, and R.F.C. Hull, *The Freud/Jung Letters: The Correspondence Between Sigmund Freud and C. G. Jung, Bollingen Series: No. 94* (Princeton, NJ, Princeton University Press, 1974).

Chapter 8

[32] Gokhan Guley and Tracey Reznik, "Culture Eats Strategy for Breakfast and Transformation for Lunch," Jabian.Journal.com, Fall, 2019, https://journal.jabian.com/culture-eats-strategy-for-breakfast-and-transformation-for-lunch/, last accessed February 10, 2022.

[33] Jesse Cole, *Find Your Yellow Tux: How to Be Successful by Standing Out* (Austin, TX: Lioncrest Publishing, 2017).

Chapter 9

[34] M. Scott Peck, *The Road Less Traveled, 25th Anniversary Edition: A New Psychology of Love, Traditional Values, and Spiritual Growth* (New York, NY: Simon and Schuster, 2003).

Chapter 10

[35] Mike Michalowicz, *Fix This Next: Make the Vital Change That Will Level Up Your Business* (New York, NY: Portfolio, 2020).

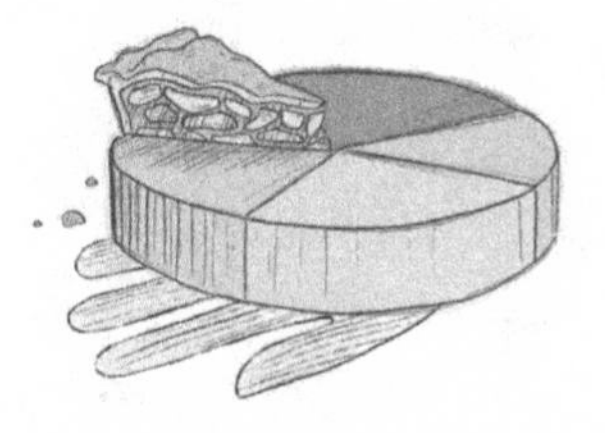

ABOUT THE AUTHOR

Cyndi Thomason is a speaker and thought leader in ecommerce accounting, and mom entrepreneurship. Through her firm, bookskeep, and her first book, *Profit First for Ecommerce Sellers,* she has helped thousands of ecommerce businesses around the world. When she is not working, you can find her in the garden, where she cultivates her own dreams both in the soil and in her heart.

ALSO BY CYNDI THOMASON

"Cyndi's knowledge of Profit First and the challenges faced by ecommerce sellers allow her to offer invaluable advice for growing while still putting money in your pocket."

—Andrew Youderian, www.eCommerceFuel.com

"The author has created a blueprint to consistent prosperity through getting a pulse on your cash flow. I am taking action on what she says and am looking forward to the process and results. Not to mention, the author actually answered my emails (unheard of) and provided amazing advice on something we were stuck on. 5 stars!"

—Destiny, Amazon 5 Star Review

Profit First for Ecommerce Sellers focuses on four critical areas that today's ecommerce sellers struggle with in growing their businesses – managing inventory; relying on debt; understanding their financial data; and maintaining focus. While the ecommerce industry presents incredible opportunities, these four areas can also present major pitfalls in the quest for success. Cyndi Thomason has taken the core concepts of the Profit First methodology and customized them to address the specific needs of the ecommerce business.

CPSIA information can be obtained
at www.ICGtesting.com
Printed in the USA
JSHW042008230322
24155JS00004B/14

9 780960 028337